MEL BAY PRESENTS

EASY UKULELE
METHOD BOOK I

BY MARY LOU DEMPLER

1 2 3 4 5 6 7 8 9 0

Visit us on the Web at www.melbay.com — E-mail us at email@melbay.com

Dear Reader,

With this Easy Ukulele Method Book, I give you a very special gift — the gift of music at your fingertips. This ukulele tablature method is so easy, in just a few minutes you will be strumming your ukulele and singing along to familiar songs. I know you will enjoy this book just as much as my students who range from the age of 4 years old to 78 years young. The ukulele is an instrument for everyone and every type of music!! Whether it's rock, country, jazz, contemporary, Christian, folk, or Hawaiian music, you can play it on the ukulele!!! I can not wait for you to discover all the wonders of this "little guitar". I truly believe *"if our eyes are windows to our souls then the ukulele is the door to our hearts!"*

Musically Yours,

Mary Lou Stout Dempler

Mary Lou Stout Dempler

Acknowledgments

I thank God for all my musical talents. My thanks and deepest appreciation to my musical soul mate and best friend Myra Jo Kean for all her help. I would like to thank and dedicate this book to my musically challenged husband Shane. Without him, I never would have discovered the ukulele, developed this easy method or have this book published.

Table of Contents

THE HISTORY OF THE UKULELE

The braguinha, a small guitar from the Portuguese island of Madeira, arrived on a boat in 1879 with 419 immigrants in Hawaii's Honolulu harbor. Joao Fernandez upon arrival began entertaining bystanders with his 4 string instrument. The islanders fell in love with the little instrument and renamed it the ukulele. Pronounced *oo-koo-le-le*, the Hawaiian name stands for "jumping flea." It was called the jumping flea because of the small fretboard. When played, fingers seem to jump from notes and chords. Another Madeirian, Manuel Nunes, exchanged the metal strings of the braguinha with gut (now nylon) strings and changed the tuning to facilitate easier chords, developing the ukulele as we now know it.

The standard ukulele tuning is G C E A, but it is sometimes tuned to A D F♯ B. The alternate tuning uses the same chord fingerings, but uses different chord names. Today, there are four sizes of ukuleles available: the Soprano (standard), the Concert, the Tenor, and the Baritone.

Hawaii invested $100,000.00 in their Pavilion at the Panama-Pacific Exposition in San Francisco in 1915. For the first time thousands of Americans heard the ukulele. The Victor Record Company sold more Hawaiian music than any other style of music in 1916. U.S. guitar companies such as Martin, Gibson, and National Resonator created their own ukulele designs that are now collectibles. Roy Smeck and Cliff Edwards (Ukulele Ike) were pop stars and great ukulele players in the 1920's. Thanks to Arthur Godfrey ukulele popularity soared in the 1940's and 1950's and millions of plastic ukuleles made by Mario Maccaferri were sold.

Now, the ukulele is popular all over the world. Hawaii hosts an annual Ukulele Festival. Japan, Canada and England are big ukulele markets as well. In the United States, we host the Ukulele Exposition, and the Ukulele Hall of Fame. Los Angeles hosts three active ukulele nightclubs. Virginia incorporates the ukulele in their elementary school curriculum and in Arkansas and Texas, there are several ukulele orchestras.

The ukulele helped to ease negotiations when diplomats and U. S. officials wore grass skirts and carried ukuleles at the Association of Southeast Asian Nations in Bruner, on August 2, 1995. Tradition requires the 14 delegations in attendance put on a musical skit. Secretary of State Warren Christopher gave the introduction and the U.S. team sang "This Land Is Your Land," with the words changed to reflect Asian politics and economy. Undersecretary of State Joan Spero carried a ukulele to the gathering in Bruner.

For a complete history, read, *The Ukulele: A Visual History* by Jim Beloff.

PARTS OF THE UKULELE

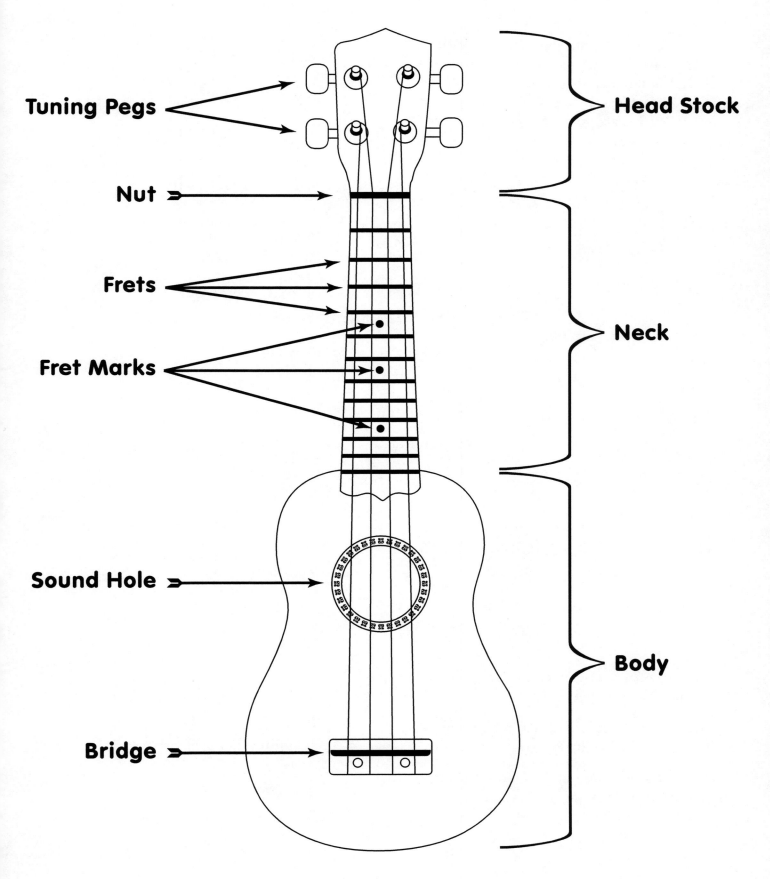

Tuning Pegs

Nut

Frets

Fret Marks

Sound Hole

Bridge

Head Stock

Neck

Body

How to Tune the Ukulele

The easiest way to tune the Ukulele is with a Uke pitch pipe. **G C E A** tuning is the most widely used tuning and is the easiest to play. This method only uses **G C E A** tuning because it is easier to play in the keys of **F**, **B♭**, **E♭**, and **A♭**. **A D F♯ B** tuning uses the same chord fingerings, but the chord names are different. Purchase a **G C E A** pitch pipe and tune to the diagram.

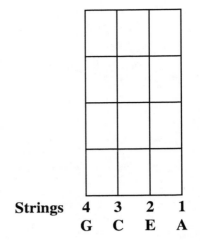

Strings 4 3 2 1
         G C E A

Tuning the Uke using a piano

begin with middle **C** for the third string

E for the second string

G for the fourth string

A for the first string.

Tuning the Uke without a pitch pipe or piano

If a pitch pipe or piano is not available, the uke can be tuned by ear. First, approximate an **A** on the first string.

Press the **fifth fret** of the second string to equal the pitch of the **first string A.**

Press the **fourth fret** of the third string to equal the pitch of the **second string E.**

Press the **second fret** of the fourth string to equal the pitch of the **first string A.**

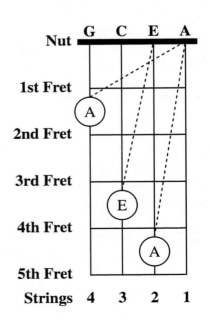

How to Hold the Uke

When playing the uke hold the head stock at the 2 o'clock position and the bottom of the body at the 7 o'clock position. Press the body of the uke firmly against your chest. Press fingers firmly on the fretboard. Do not touch the strings when forming left hand finger positions for notes or chords.

Hand and Finger Positions for the Uke

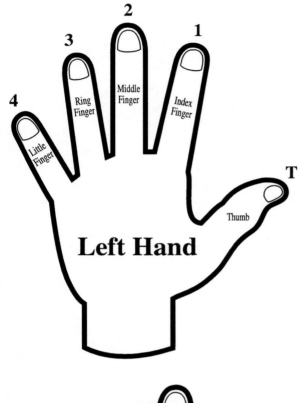

The left hand holds the neck of the uke. The thumb is behind the neck, wrist relaxed, and hand is arched over the strings.

The **first finger** (index) plays notes on the **first fret.**

The **second finger** (middle) plays notes on the **second fret.**

The **third finger** (ring) plays notes on the **third fret.**

The **fourth finger** (little) plays notes on the **fourth fret.**

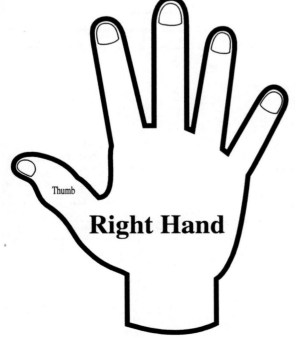

The right hand strums the strings. Use a pick or the thumb to strum. A down stroke is indicated with the symbol ⊓ (down stroke). An up stroke is indicated with the symbol V (up stroke).

Basics of Music

The Staff

Music is written on a *staff.* A staff has five lines and four spaces. The lines are labeled **E, G, B, D,** and **F.** Memory aid: *"Every Good Boy Does Fine."*

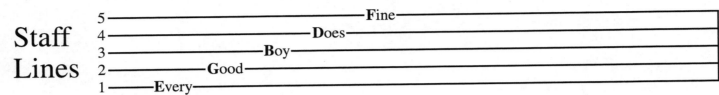

Staff Lines

The spaces are labeled **F, A, C,** and **E.** Memory aid: *"Face."*

Staff Spaces

The Staff begins with a *Treble Clef.*

The Staff is divided into *Measures* by lines called *Barlines.*

Double Barlines indicate the end of a section. *Final Barlines* indicate the end of a piece.

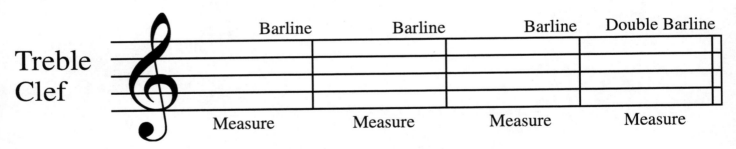

Treble Clef

Double Barlines with Dots indicate that this section of music is repeated.

When you see a backward repeat, go back to the previous forward repeat. If there isn't a forward repeat in the measures before the backward repeat, go back to the beginning of the piece.

Time Signature

The *time signature* is placed after the clef. It denotes the rhythm of the music.

The *top number* is the number of beats per measure.

The *bottom number* is the type of note that receives one beat.

Time Signature

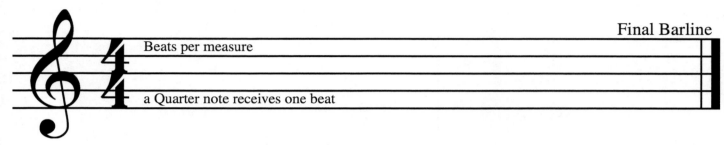

In four-four time, there will be four beats per measure

Time Signature - C is another way of writing four-four time, and is called *"Common Time."*

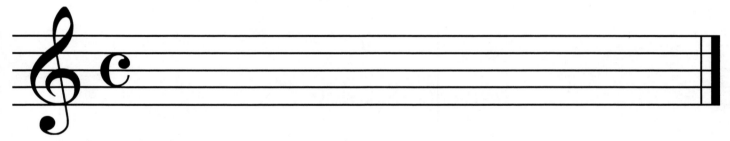

Time Signature

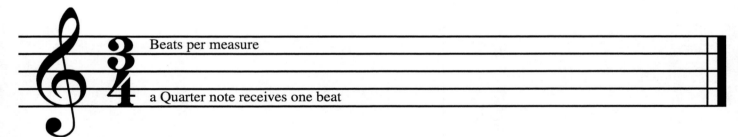

In three-four time, there will be three beats per measure.

Time Signature

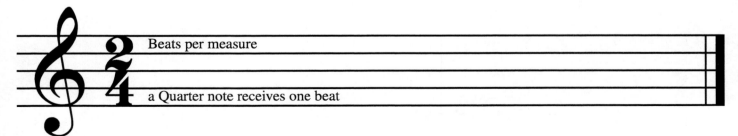

In two-four time, there will be two beats per measure.

Notes

Notes on a line or space of the staff carry the name of that line or space.

Staff

5 ——————Fine——————	4		E	
4 ————————Does————	3		C	
3 ——————Boy————————	2	A		
2 ————Good——————————	1	F		● (This is an **F** note)
1 —Every————————————				

Note	Name	Beats	Description
o	Whole Note	4	Hollow Head
♩ (hollow)	Half Note	2	Hollow head and stem.
♩· (hollow)	Dotted Half Note	3	Hollow head, stem and a dot to the right of the note head.
♩	Quarter Note	1	Solid head and stem.
♩·	Dotted Quarter Note	1½	Solid head, stem and a dot to the right of the note head.
♪	Eighth Note	½	Solid head, stem and flag.
♫	Two Eighth Notes	1	Two eighth notes are connected by a beam.

Ledger Lines

When the pitch of a note is below or above the staff, notes are on or between the lines called *Ledger Lines*.

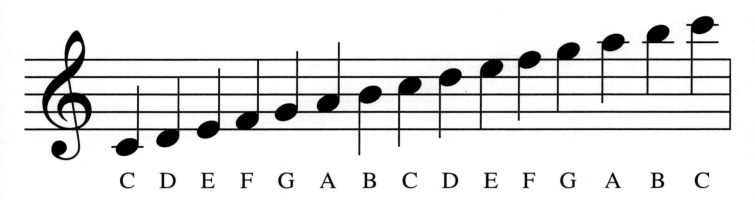

C D E F G A B C D E F G A B C

Sharps, Flats and Naturals

The symbol for a sharp is ♯. It is placed before a note, and raises the note 1/2 step, which is one fret toward the bridge.

The symbol for a flat is ♭. It is placed before a note, and lowers the note 1/2 step, which is one fret toward the nut.

The symbol for a natural is ♮. It is placed before a note, and cancels the previous sharp (♯) or flat (♭).

Key Signature

On the staff after the treble clef and before the time signature is the *Key Signature*. It indicates any notes which are played with a sharp or flat through the music. In this example, the sharp on the F line means that any F note is sharped throughout the music, unless preceded by the natural (♮) symbol.

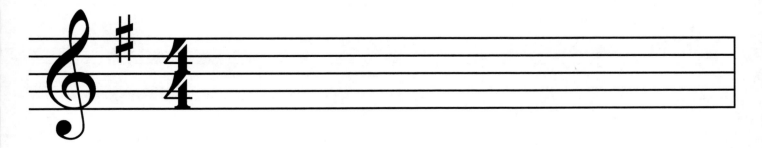

The Tie

Two notes of the same pitch may be connected with a curved line called a *Tie*. The first note is played and held for the count of both notes. The second note is held, *not played*.

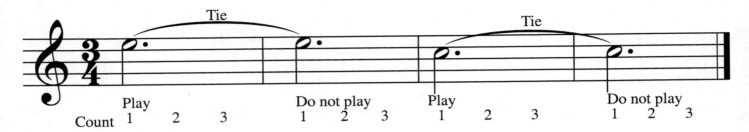

Pick-Up Notes

Notes before the first measure are called *Pick-Up Notes*. They are taken from the last measure of the song and the beats are counted as the end of a measure.

Rests

Symbols called *Rests* denote silent periods. The silent period is the same amount of time as the corresponding notes.

How to Read Tablature

Tablature is a simple diagram of the ukulele fretboard. The lines in tablature represent each string. The number on the string indicates the fret that is played on that string to sound the note written on the staff. In the example above, the first measure of the staff contains four A notes. The tablature example below the staff indicates the position of the A notes. Play the first string 0 (0 = open, do not finger any fret) four times. The bar lines that separate the measures of the tablature correspond with the bar lines on the music staff. The second measure contains four B notes found on the first string, at the second fret, played four times. The third measure is four C notes, found on the first string, at the third fret, played four times. Tablature is not a substitute for the staff. It is a diagram (map) to locate notes on the ukulele fretboard.

First (A) String Notes
Quarter Notes

Half Notes

Whole Notes

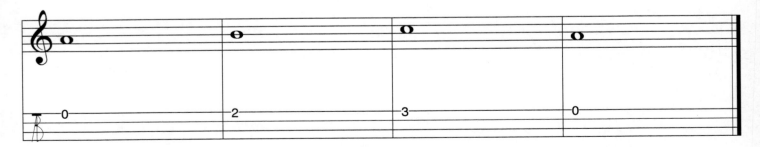

First (A) String Melody

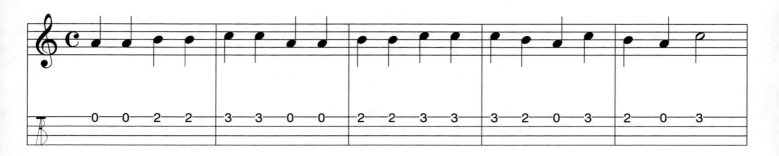

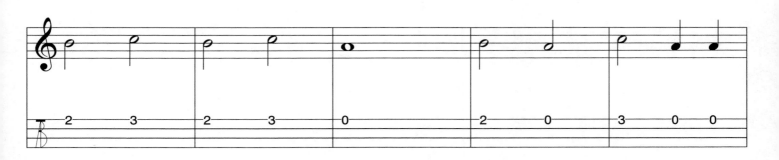

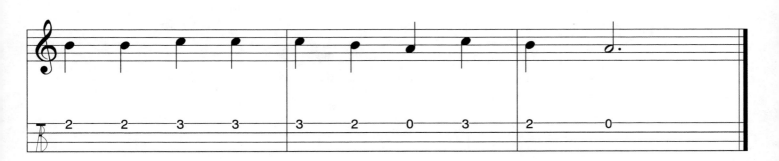

15

Chord Diagrams C and G7

In order to play a chord, place your fingers as indicated on the chord diagram. The strings are the vertical lines and ther frets are the horzontal lines. The circles with numbers indicate the position of the left hand fingers. Place fingers firmly on the fret to produce a clear sound. Do not place fingers directly on top of the fret bar. Open strings require no fingers on the fret board. Open strings are represented by the circles below the string numbers.

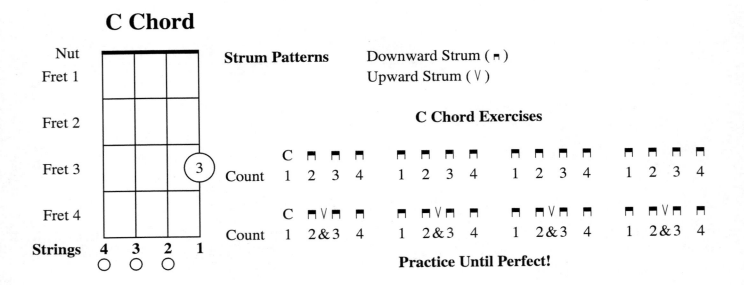

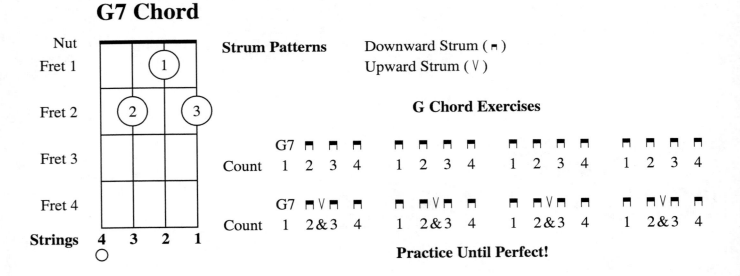

Three Blind Mice

Anonymous

Practice strumming and singing with these songs. Use the tablature to find melody notes.

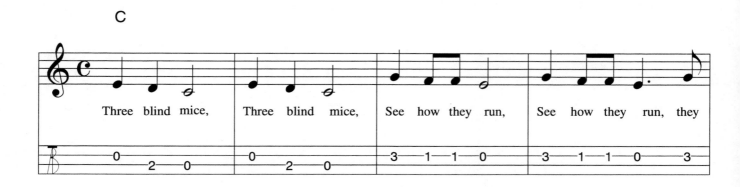

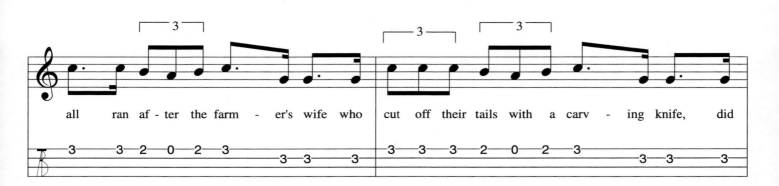

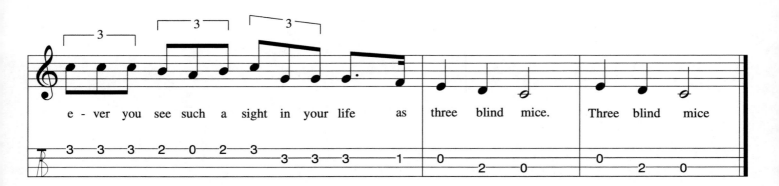

Note: Second string notes are explained on page 23. Third string notes are explained on page 32.

Row, Row, Row Your Boat

Traditional

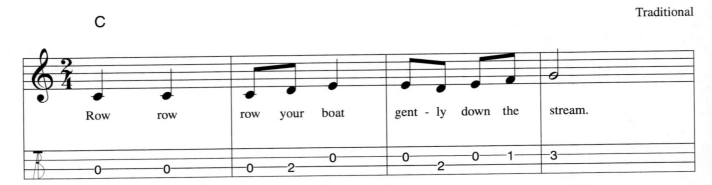

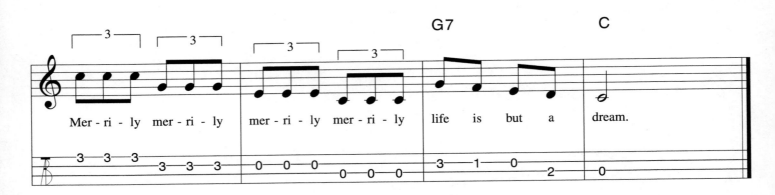

This page has been left blank
to avoid awkward page turns.

This Old Man

Anonymous

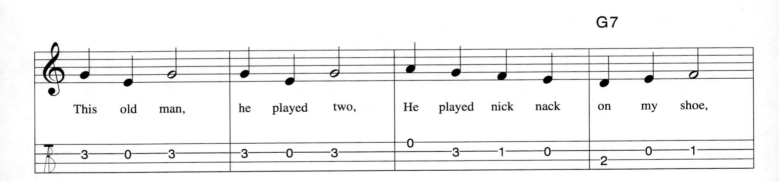

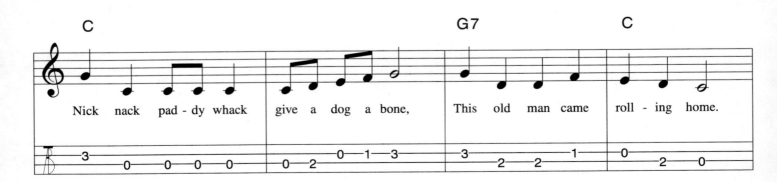

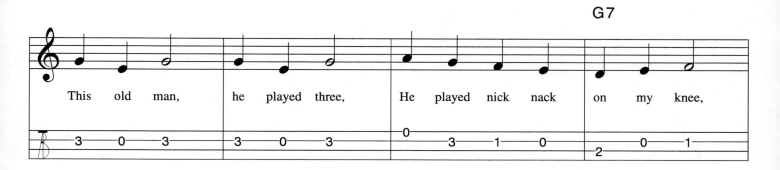

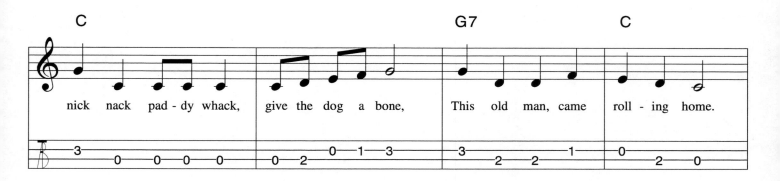

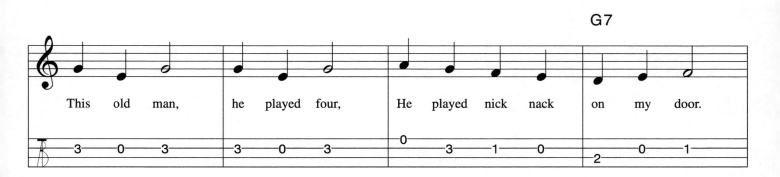

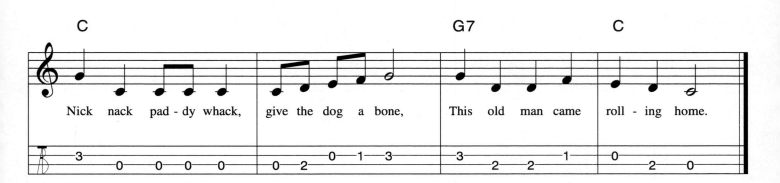

Skip to My Lou

Traditional

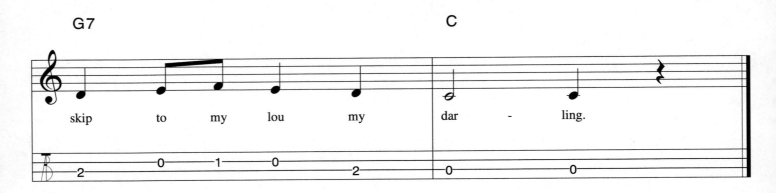

Second (E) String Notes

Quarter Notes

Half Notes

Whole Notes

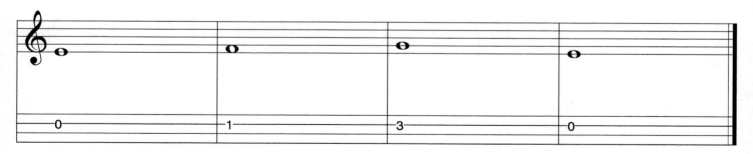

23

Second (E) String Melody

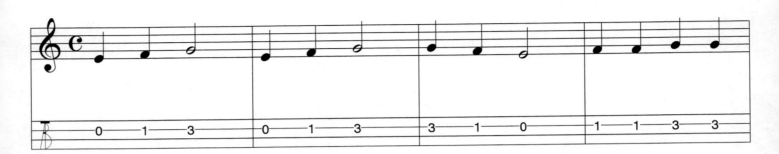

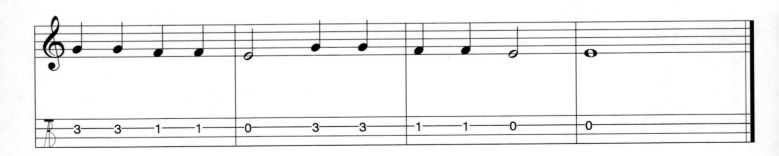

24

A and E String Melody

Chord Diagrams F and C7

F Chord

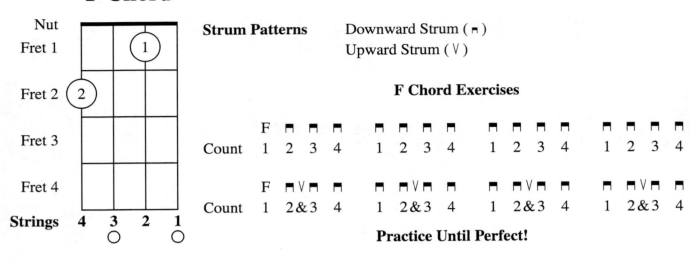

Nut
Fret 1
Fret 2
Fret 3
Fret 4
Strings 4 3 2 1

Strum Patterns   Downward Strum (⊓)
                     Upward Strum (V)

F Chord Exercises

	F	⊓	⊓	⊓	⊓	⊓	⊓	⊓	⊓	⊓	⊓	⊓	⊓	⊓	⊓	⊓
Count	1	2	3	4	1	2	3	4	1	2	3	4	1	2	3	4
	F	⊓	V	⊓	⊓	⊓	⊓	V	⊓	⊓	⊓	⊓	V	⊓	⊓	⊓	⊓	V	⊓	⊓
Count	1	2 & 3	4	1	2 & 3	4	1	2 & 3	4	1	2 & 3	4

Practice Until Perfect!

C7 Chord

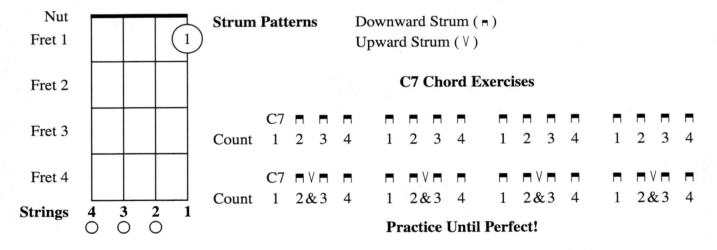

Nut
Fret 1
Fret 2
Fret 3
Fret 4
Strings 4 3 2 1

Strum Patterns   Downward Strum (⊓)
                     Upward Strum (V)

C7 Chord Exercises

	C7	⊓	⊓	⊓	⊓	⊓	⊓	⊓	⊓	⊓	⊓	⊓	⊓	⊓	⊓	⊓
Count	1	2	3	4	1	2	3	4	1	2	3	4	1	2	3	4
	C7	⊓	V	⊓	⊓	⊓	⊓	V	⊓	⊓	⊓	⊓	V	⊓	⊓	⊓	⊓	V	⊓	⊓
Count	1	2 & 3	4	1	2 & 3	4	1	2 & 3	4	1	2 & 3	4

Practice Until Perfect!

Are You Sleeping

Traditional Folk Song
from France

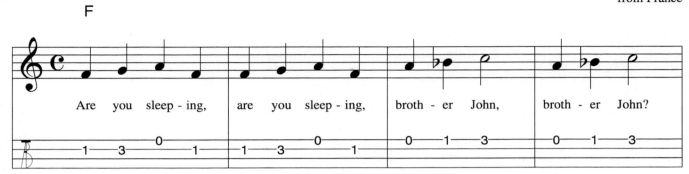

Ten Little Indians

Septimus Winner

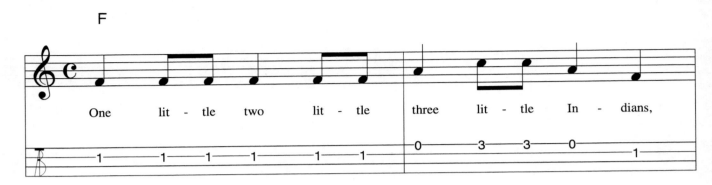

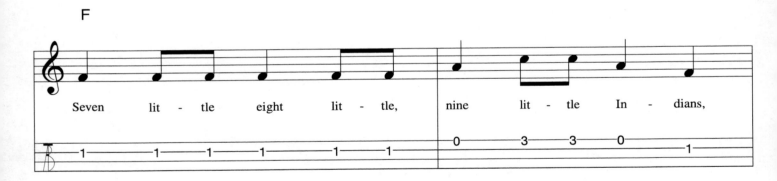

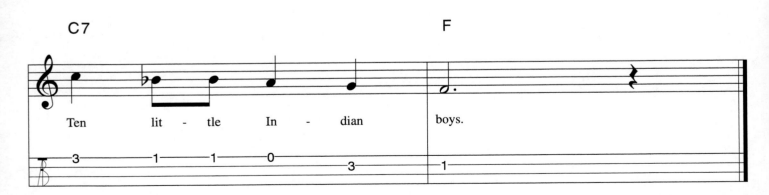

London Bridge

Traditional Children's Song from England

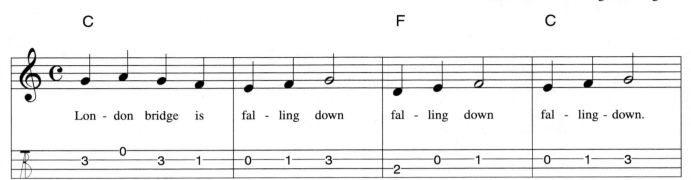

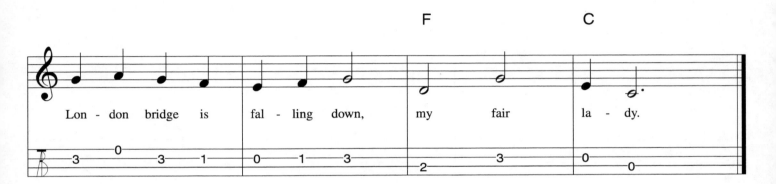

Twinkle, Twinkle, Little Star

Words by Jane Taylor

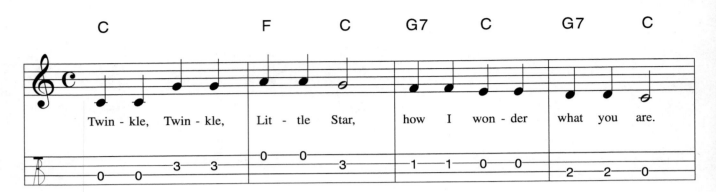

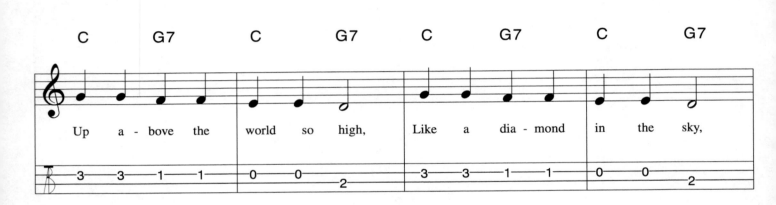

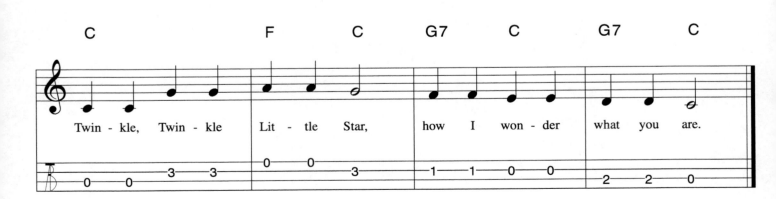

Camptown Races

Words and Music by
Stephen Collins Foster

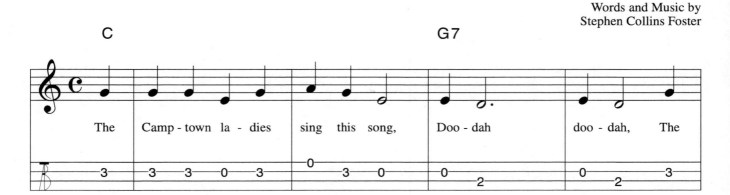

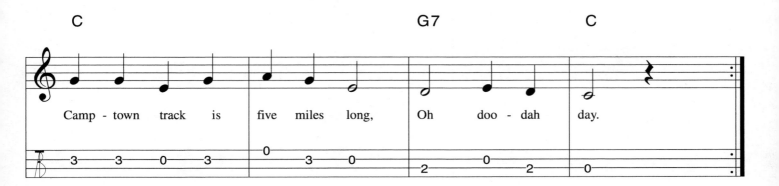

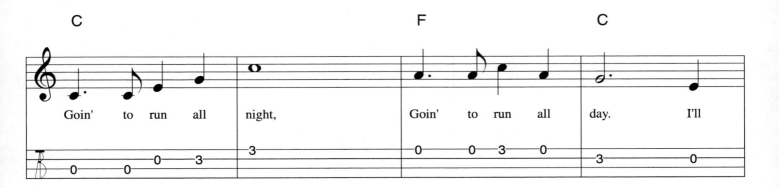

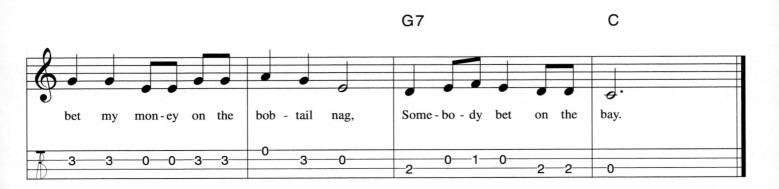

Third (C) String Notes

Quarter Notes

Half Notes

Whole Notes

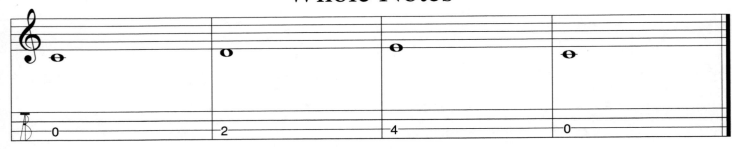

Third (C) String Melody

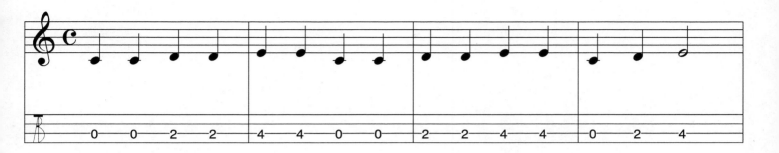

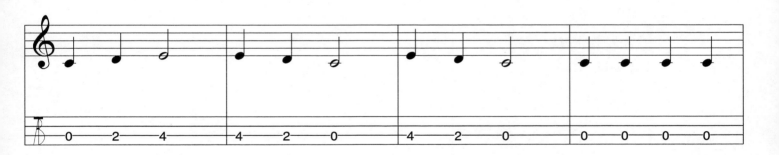

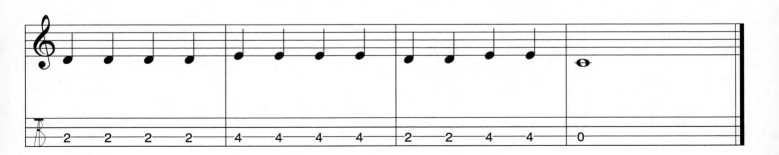

* Now that you know the notes on the first three strings, you should go back and review the earlier songs, playing the melody.

33

Chord Diagrams G and D7

G Chord

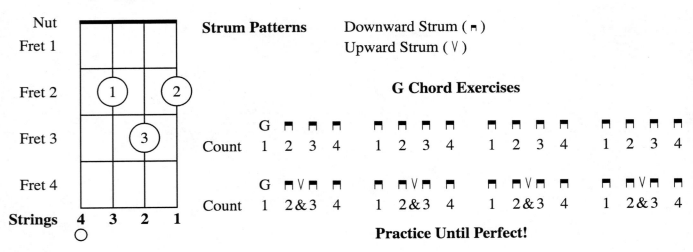

Nut			
Fret 1			
Fret 2	①		②
Fret 3		③	
Fret 4			
Strings	4 3 2 1		

Strum Patterns   Downward Strum (⊓)
Upward Strum (V)

G Chord Exercises

G ⊓ ⊓ ⊓   ⊓ ⊓ ⊓ ⊓   ⊓ ⊓ ⊓ ⊓   ⊓ ⊓ ⊓ ⊓
Count 1 2 3 4   1 2 3 4   1 2 3 4   1 2 3 4

G ⊓ V ⊓ ⊓   ⊓ ⊓ V ⊓ ⊓   ⊓ ⊓ V ⊓ ⊓   ⊓ ⊓ V ⊓ ⊓
Count 1 2&3 4   1 2&3 4   1 2&3 4   1 2&3 4

Practice Until Perfect!

D7 Chord

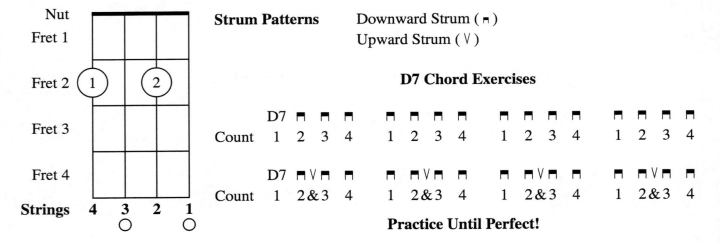

Nut			
Fret 1			
Fret 2	①		②
Fret 3			
Fret 4			
Strings	4 3 2 1		

Strum Patterns   Downward Strum (⊓)
Upward Strum (V)

D7 Chord Exercises

D7 ⊓ ⊓ ⊓   ⊓ ⊓ ⊓ ⊓   ⊓ ⊓ ⊓ ⊓   ⊓ ⊓ ⊓ ⊓
Count 1 2 3 4   1 2 3 4   1 2 3 4   1 2 3 4

D7 ⊓ V ⊓ ⊓   ⊓ ⊓ V ⊓ ⊓   ⊓ ⊓ V ⊓ ⊓   ⊓ ⊓ V ⊓ ⊓
Count 1 2&3 4   1 2&3 4   1 2&3 4   1 2&3 4

Practice Until Perfect!

Old MacDonald Had a Farm

English words by
Thomas D'Vrfey

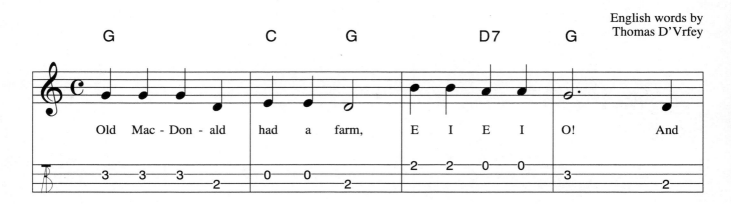

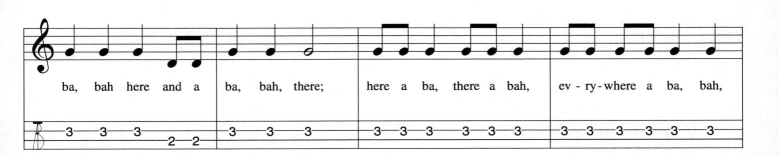

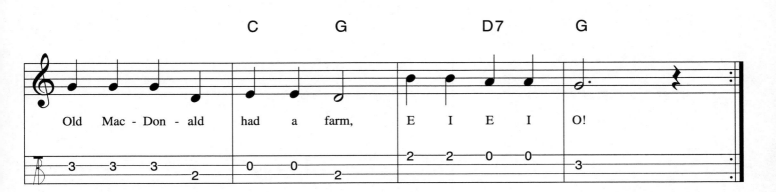

When the Saints Go Marching In

Spiritual
Words by Katherine E. Purvis
Music by James M. Black

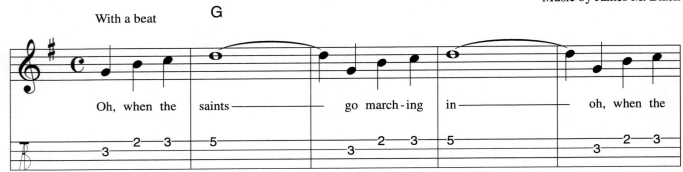

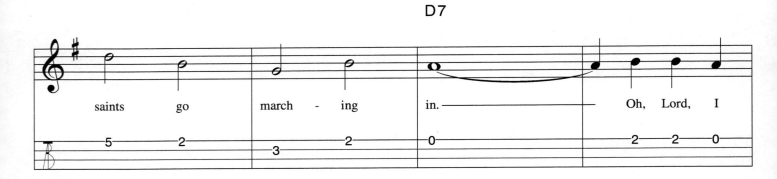

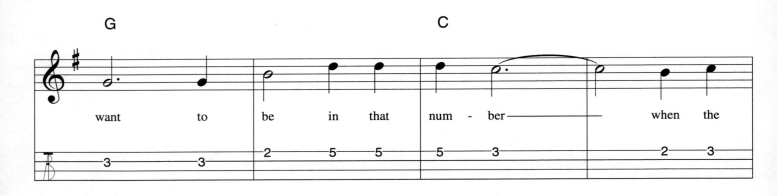

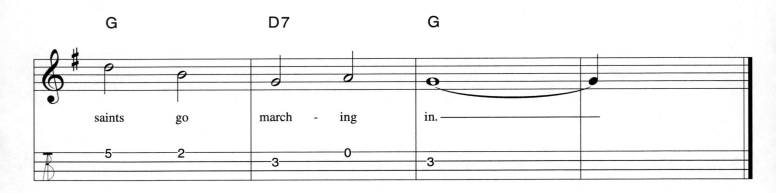

He's Got the Whole World in His Hands

Traditional Black
American Spiritual

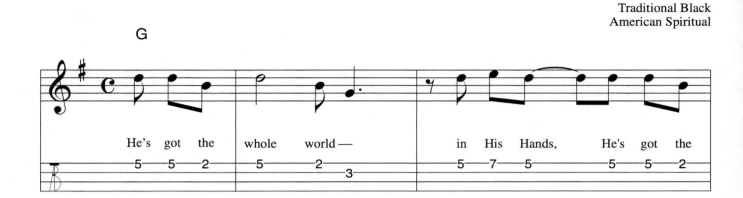

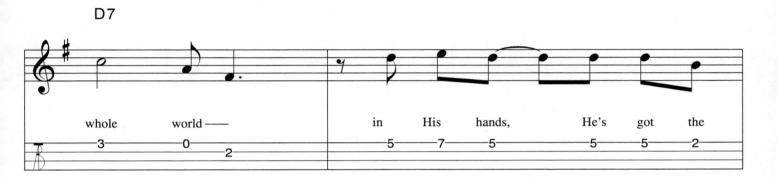

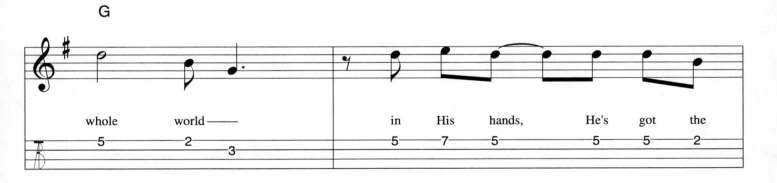

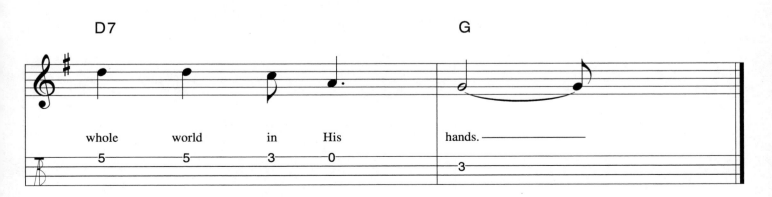

Will the Circle Be Unbroken

Traditional Gospel

Words by Ada R. Habershon
Music by Charles H. Gabriel

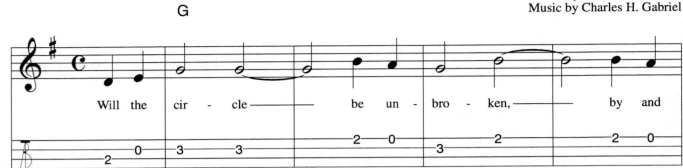

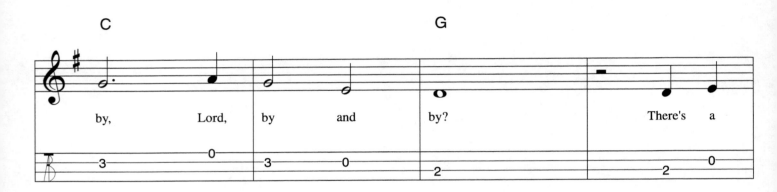

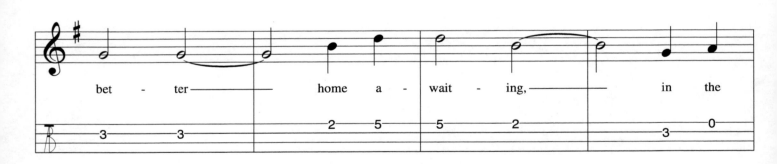

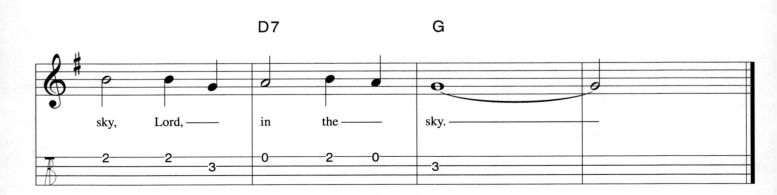

Fourth (G) String Notes

Quarter Notes

Half Notes

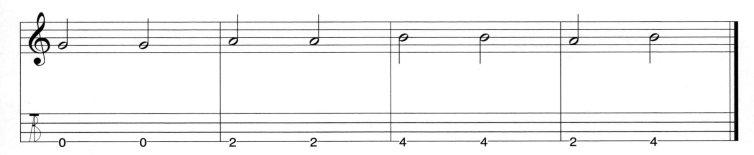

Whole Notes

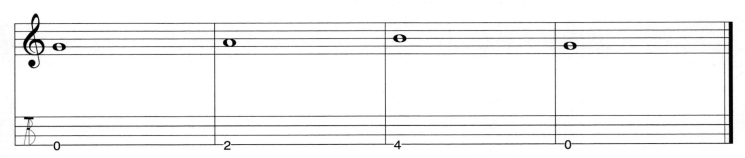

Fourth (G) String Melody

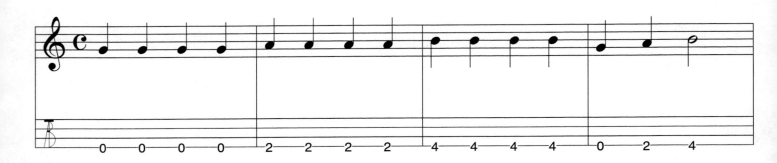

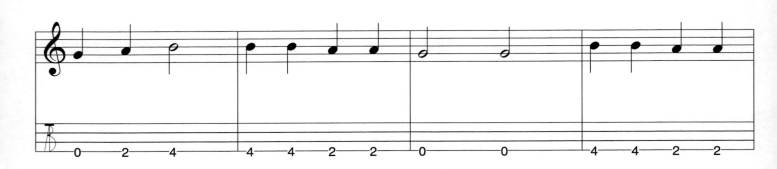

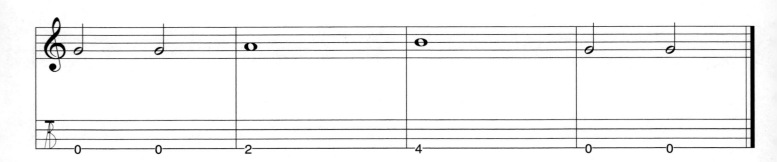

Chord Diagrams B-flat and D

B♭ Chord

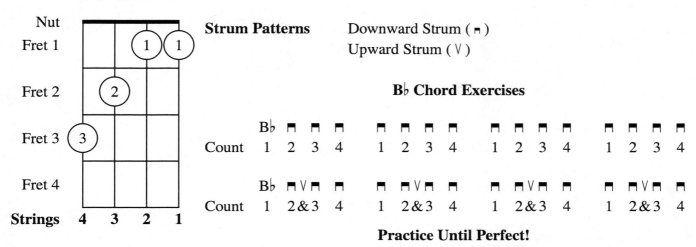

D Chord

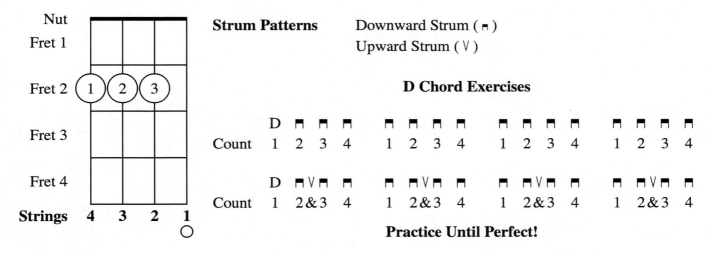

This Train

Tablature Arrangement
Mary Lou Dempler

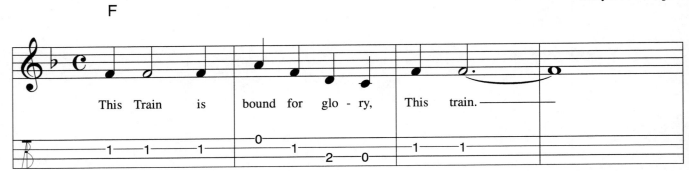

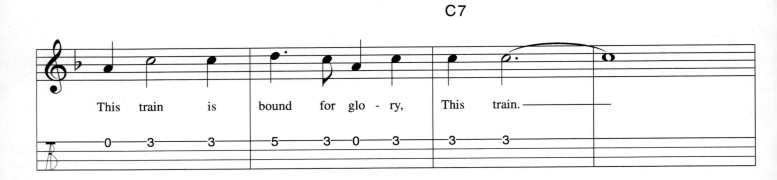

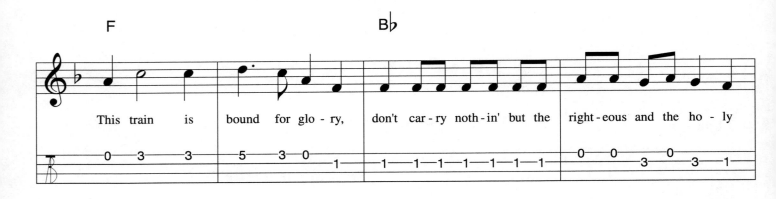

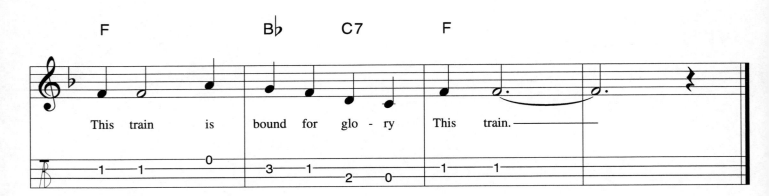

Amazing Grace

Traditional

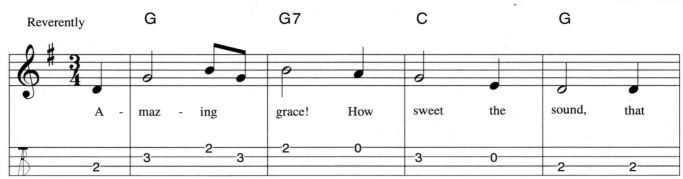

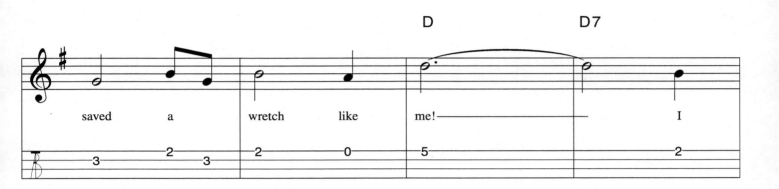

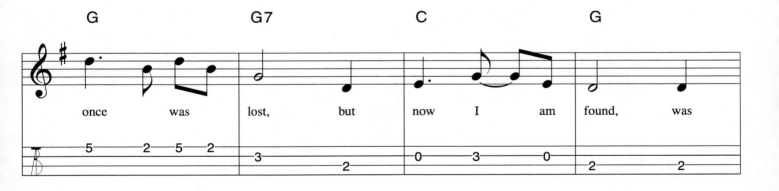

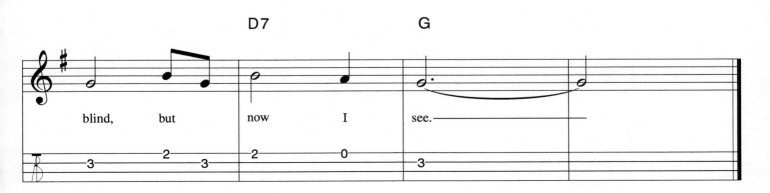

Away in a Manger

Words-Anonymous
Music-James Ramsey Murray

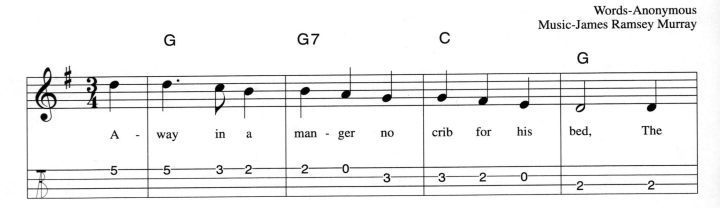

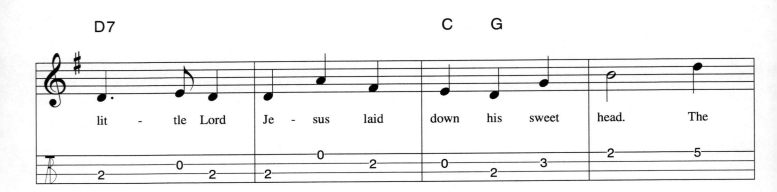

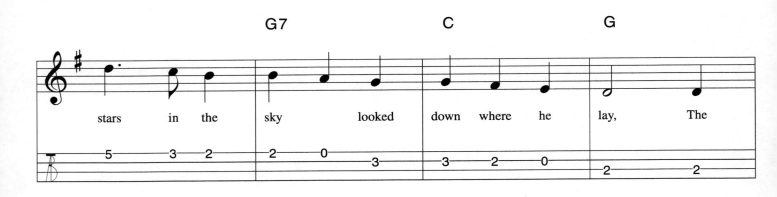

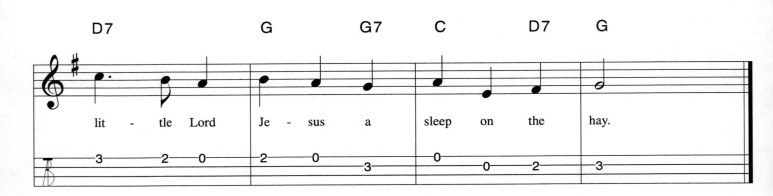

Silent Night

German Words Joseph Mohr
English Words Anonymous
Music by Franz Gruber

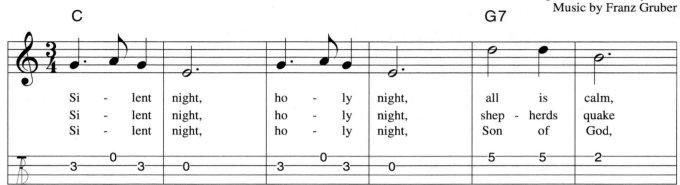

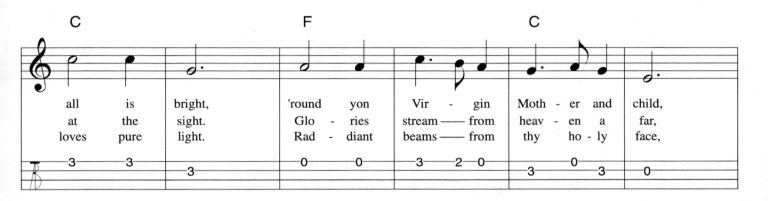

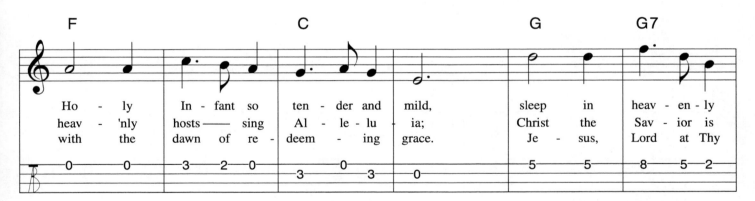

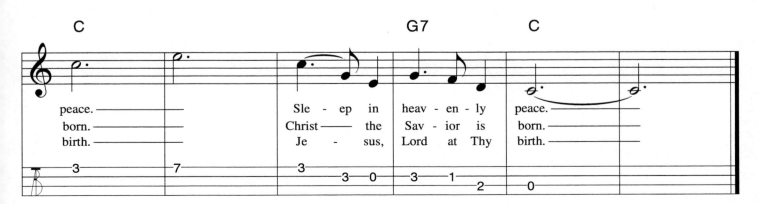

Chord Chart

C Chord
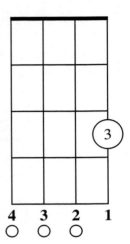

F Chord
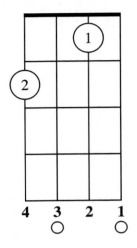

G Chord
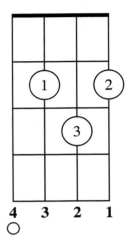

B♭ Chord
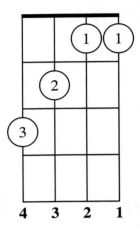

G7 Chord
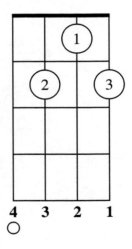

C7 Chord
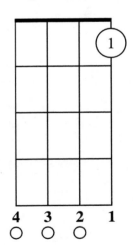

D7 Chord
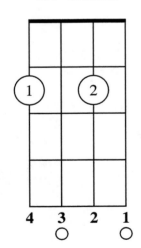

D Chord
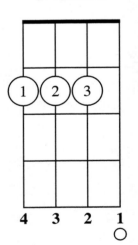

About the Author

Mary Lou Stout Dempler, a professional musician, began her musical career at age seven at the Ursuline School of Music and Drama in Louisville, Kentucky, where she studied guitar. She continued to study Jazz guitar after high school at Bellarmine University. In addition to a 20 year teaching career, in 1997 she was the recipient of the Duesquene University Scholarship for only 50 guitar instructors from across the nation. In 1998, her husband Shane had a ukulele custom designed and hand made for her birthday. Mary Lou fell in love with its gentle harp-like sound and in the fall of 1998, she received an invitation to attend a ukulele workshop at Harvard University and became a member of The Ukulele Hall of Fame. She created the ukulele tablature method and wrote the *Easy Ukulele Method Book I,* and *Easy Ukulele Method Book II.* Her method books are designed for anyone, regardless of their musical background, to immediately enjoy playing music on the ukulele. She is a member of the faculty at Bellarmine University where she teaches several different ukulele classes. Because of her love of the ukulele and the desire to share the joy of this instrument with everyone, she founded a ukulele orchestra, **The Louisville Ukulele Association Unlimited (LUAU).** Mary Lou formed the musical duo **The Unique Ukuleles,** in an effort to promote ukulele music and showcase the instrument's versatility by performing rock, swing, jazz, folk, country, Christian and contemporary music. The Unique Ukuleles have recorded two albums, *Unique Ukulele Christmas* and *Songs from the Heart.* She truly believes, "If our eyes are the windows to our souls, then the ukulele is the door to our hearts!"

THE 6 CHORD SONGBOOK

The 'Bob Dylan 6 Chord Songbook' allows eve
play and enjoy the magic of Dylan's music. By le
will soon master 20 of his be:
The 'Bob Dylan 6 Chord Songbook' does not use musical notation. All you
need to learn is 6 chords and their symbols. The chord boxes are printed on
each page to remind you, and the chord changes are shown above the lyrics.
If you find the pitch of a song outside your vocal range, simply place your
capo behind a suitable fret and use the same chord shapes! The strum
rhythm or picking pattern most suited to the song is left for you to decide.
The 'Bob Dylan 6 Chord Songbook' guarantees hours of enjoyment for
guitarists of all levels, as well as providing a fine basis for
building a strong repertoire.
When you have mastered the first 6 chords, you will want to progress to use
more chords with these songs. These are described within the text and
illustrated in a comprehensive Chord Glossary at the back of the book.

Exclusive Distributors:
Music Sales Limited
8/9 Frith Street, London, W1V 5TZ, England
Music Sales Corporation
257 Park Avenue South, New York, NY10010, USA.
Music Sales Pty. Limited
120 Rothschild Avenue, Rosebery, NSW 2018, Australia

This book © Copyright 1991 by Special Rider Music
Order No. AM78924
UK ISBN 0.7119.2183.0
US ISBN 0.8256.2614.5

Book design by Pearce Marchbank Studio
Song pages setting by MSS Studios
Arranged by Rick Cardinali
Cover photography Ken Regan

Your Guarantee of Quality
As publishers, we strive to produce every book to the
highest commercial standards.
Particular care has been given to specifying acid-free, neutral-sized paper which has not
been elemental chlorine bleached but produced with special regard for the environment.
Throughout, the printing and binding have been planned to ensure a sturdy, attractive
publication which should give years of enjoyment.
If your copy fails to meet our high standards, please inform us and we will gladly replace it.

Music Sales' complete catalogue lists thousands of titles and is
free from your local music book shop, or direct from Music Sales Limited. Please send a cheque
or postal order for £1.50 for postage to
Music Sales Limited, Newmarket Road, Bury St Edmunds, Suffolk IP33 3YB.

Printed and bound in Great Britain by
Caligraving Limited Thetford Norfolk

Wise Publications
London/New York/Sydney

Knockin' On Heaven's Door

Words & Music by Bob Dylan

```
  C              G           Dm
  Mama, take this badge off me,
  C        G          F
  I can't use it anymore.
  C            G            Dm
  It's gettin' dark, too dark for me to see,
  C            G                       F
  I feel like I'm knockin' on heaven's door.
```

Chorus

```
  C              G                Dm
  Knock, knock, knockin' on heaven's door,
  C              G                F
  Knock, knock, knockin' on heaven's door,
  C              G                Dm
  Knock, knock, knockin' on heaven's door,
  C              G                F
  Knock, knock, knockin' on heaven's door.
```

```
  C              G                Dm
  Mama, put my guns in the ground,
  C        G              F
  I can't shoot them any more.
  C              G                Dm
  That long black cloud is comin' down,
  C            G                       F
  I feel like I'm knockin' on heaven's door.
```

Chorus

```
  C              G
  Knock, knock, knockin' ....
```

Repeat and fade
```
C  G  Dm      C  G  Dm
```

C   F   Am   G   Em   Dm

All Along The Watchtower

Words & Music by Bob Dylan

Am   **F**   **G**
"There must be some way out of here,"

Am   **F**   **G**
Said the joker to the thief,

Am   **F**   **G**
"There's too much confusion,

Am   **F**   **G**
I can't get no relief."

Am   **F**   **G**
"Business men, they drink my wine,

Am   **F**   **G**
Plowmen dig my earth,

Am   **F**   **G**
None of them along the line

Am   **F**   **G**
Know what any of it is worth."

Am   **F**   **G**
"No reason to get excited,"

Am   **F**   **G**
The thief, he kindly spoke,

Am   **F**   **G**
"There are many here among us

Am   **F**   **G**
Who feel that life is but a joke.

Am   **F**   **G**
But you and I, we've been thru that,

Am   **F**   **G**
And this is not our fate,

Am   **F**   **G**
So let us not talk falsely now,

Am   **F**   **G**
The hour is getting late."

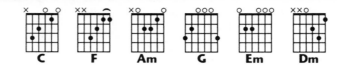

Am   F   G
   All along the watchtower,
Am   F   G
   Princes kept the view
Am   F   G
   While all the women came and went,
Am   F   G
   Barefoot servants, too.
Am   F   G
   Outside in the distance
Am   F   G
   A wildcat did growl,
Am   F   G
   Two riders were approaching,
Am   F   G Am
   The wind began to howl.

The Mighty Quinn

Words & Music by Bob Dylan

C   F   C   F
   Ev'rybody's building the big ships and the boats,
C   F
   Some are building monuments,
C   F
   Others jotting down notes.
C   F
   Ev'rybody's in despair,
C   F
   Ev'ry girl and boy but when
   C   G
   Quinn The Eskimo gets here,
   F   C
   Ev'rybody's gonna jump for joy.

Chorus

   C   G   C
   Come all without, come all within,
        G   F   C
   You'll not see nothing like the mighty Quinn.
   C   G   C
   Come all without, come on within,
        G   F   C
   You'll not see nothing like the mighty Quinn.

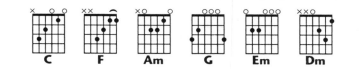

C   F   C   F
I like to do just like the rest, I like my sugar sweet,

  C   F
But guarding fumes and making haste,

 C   F
It ain't my cup of meat.

C   F
Ev'rybody's 'neath the trees,

   C   F
Feeding pigeons on a limb

    C   G
But when Quinn The Eskimo gets here,

   F   C
All the pigeons' gonna run to him.

Chorus

C   G
Come all without ....

C   F   C   F
A cat's meow and a cow's moo, I can recite 'em all;

   C   F
Just tell me where it hurts yuh, honey,

   C   F
And I'll tell you who to call.

C   F
Nobody can get no sleep,

   C   F
There's someone on ev'ryone's toes,

   C   G
But when Quinn the Eskimo gets here,

  F   C
Ev'rybody's gonna wanna doze.

Chorus

C   G
Come all without ....

(Instrumental)   C G F C

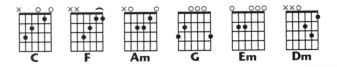

Hurricane

Music by Bob Dylan
Words by Bob Dylan & Jacques Levy

Am   **F**
Pistol shots ring out in the barroom night,

Am   **F**
Enter Patty Valentine from the upper hall.

Am   **F**
She sees the bartender in a pool of blood,

Am   **F**
Cries out, "My God, they killed them all!"

C   **F**
Here comes the story of the Hurricane,

C   **F**
The man the authorities came to blame

Dm   **C**
For somethin' that he never done.

Dm   **C**   **Em**   **Am**
Put in a prison cell, but one time he coulda been

    F   **C**   **G**   **Am**   **F**   **Am**   **F**
The champion of the world.

Am   **F**
Three bodies lyin' there does Patty see,

    Am   **F**
And another man named Bello, movin' around mysteriously.

Am   **F**
"I didn't do it," he says, and he throws up his hands,

   Am   **F**   **C**
"I was only robbin' the register, I hope you understand.

    F   **C**
I saw them leavin'," he says, and he stops,

    F
"One of us had better call up the cops".

Dm   **C**
And so Patty calls the cops,

Dm   **C**   **Em**   **Am**
And they arrive on the scene with their red lights flashin',

    F   **C**   **G**   **Am**   **F**   **Am**   **F**
In the hot New Jersey night.

Am   **F**
Meanwhile, far away in another part of town

   Am   **F**
Rubin Carter and a couple of friends are drivin' around.

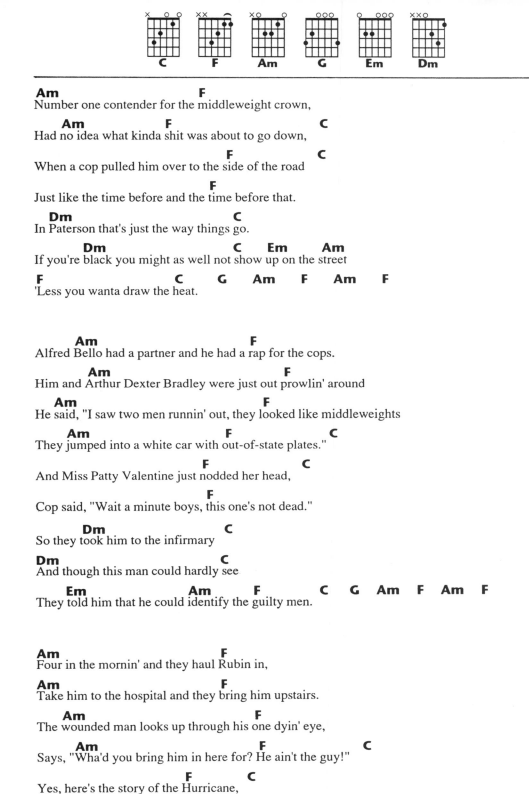

C   **F**   **Am**   **G**   **Em**   **Dm**

Am   **F**
Number one contender for the middleweight crown,

    Am   **F**   **C**
Had no idea what kinda shit was about to go down,

                    F   **C**
When a cop pulled him over to the side of the road

                   F
Just like the time before and the time before that.

  Dm   **C**
In Paterson that's just the way things go.

       Dm   **C**   **Em**   **Am**
If you're black you might as well not show up on the street

F   **C**   **G**   **Am** **F** **Am**   **F**
'Less you wanta draw the heat.

     Am   **F**
Alfred Bello had a partner and he had a rap for the cops.

     Am   **F**
Him and Arthur Dexter Bradley were just out prowlin' around

  Am   **F**
He said, "I saw two men runnin' out, they looked like middleweights

    Am   **F**   **C**
They jumped into a white car with out-of-state plates."

                F   **C**
And Miss Patty Valentine just nodded her head,

               F
Cop said, "Wait a minute boys, this one's not dead."

    Dm   **C**
So they took him to the infirmary

Dm   **C**
And though this man could hardly see

   Em   **Am**   **F**   **C** **G** **Am** **F** **Am** **F**
They told him that he could identify the guilty men.

Am   **F**
Four in the mornin' and they haul Rubin in,

Am   **F**
Take him to the hospital and they bring him upstairs.

    Am   **F**
The wounded man looks up through his one dyin' eye,

     Am   **F**   **C**
Says, "Wha'd you bring him in here for? He ain't the guy!"

               F   **C**
Yes, here's the story of the Hurricane,

               F   **Dm**
The man the authorities came to blame

             C   **Dm**
For somethin' that he never done.

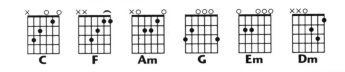

C Em   Am
Put in a prison cell, but one time he coulda been

   F   C   G   Am F Am F
The champion of the world.

Am   F
Four months later, the ghettoes are in flame,

Am   F
Rubin's in South America, fightin' for his name.

    Am   F
While Arthur Dexter Bradley's still in the robbery game,

      Am   F   C
And the cops are puttin' the screws to him, lookin' for somebody to blame.

                   F
"Remember that murder that happened in a bar?"

C   F
"Remember you said you saw the getaway car?"

     Dm   C
"You think you'd like to play ball with the law?"

Dm   C Em   Am
"Think it mighta been that fighter that you saw runnin' that night?"

    F   C   G   Am F Am F
"Don't forget that you are white."

Am   F
Arthur Dexter Bradley said, "I'm really not sure."

Am   F
Cops said, "A poor boy like you could use a break

    Am   F
We got you for the motel job and we're talkin' to your friend Bello

     Am   F   C
Now you don't wanta have to go back to jail, be a nice fellow.

        F   C
You'll be doin' society a favor.

         F   Dm
That sonofabitch is brave and gettin' braver.

            C   Dm
We want to put his ass in stir

            C Em Am
We want to pin this triple murder on him

    F   C   G   Am F Am F
He ain't no Gentleman Jim."

Am   F
Rubin could take a man out with just one punch

    Am   F
But he never did like to talk about it all that much.

     Am   F
It's my work, he'd say, and I do it for pay,

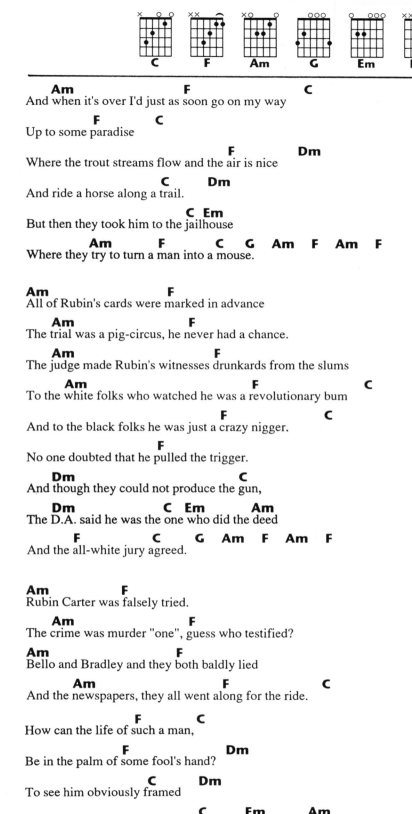

    C   F   Am   G   Em   Dm

Am   **F**   **C**
And when it's over I'd just as soon go on my way

       F   **C**
Up to some paradise

                    F   **Dm**
Where the trout streams flow and the air is nice

                C   **Dm**
And ride a horse along a trail.

                  C Em
But then they took him to the jailhouse

      Am   **F**   **C G Am F Am F**
Where they try to turn a man into a mouse.

Am   **F**
All of Rubin's cards were marked in advance

   Am   **F**
The trial was a pig-circus, he never had a chance.

   Am   **F**
The judge made Rubin's witnesses drunkards from the slums

    Am   **F**   **C**
To the white folks who watched he was a revolutionary bum

                 F   **C**
And to the black folks he was just a crazy nigger.

           F
No one doubted that he pulled the trigger.

 Dm   **C**
And though they could not produce the gun,

 Dm   **C Em**   **Am**
The D.A. said he was the one who did the deed

    F   **C**   **G Am F Am F**
And the all-white jury agreed.

Am   **F**
Rubin Carter was falsely tried.

  Am   **F**
The crime was murder "one", guess who testified?

Am   **F**
Bello and Bradley and they both baldly lied

   Am   **F**   **C**
And the newspapers, they all went along for the ride.

      F   **C**
How can the life of such a man,

      F   **Dm**
Be in the palm of some fool's hand?

        C   **Dm**
To see him obviously framed

          C   **Em**   **Am**
Couldn't help but make me feel ashamed to live in a land

   F   **C**   **G Am F Am F**
Where justice is a game.

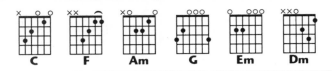

C	F	Am	G	Em	Dm

Am   **F**
Now all the criminals in their coats and their ties

Am   **F**
Are free to drink martinis and watch the sun rise

Am   **F**
While Rubin sits like Buddha in a ten-foot cell

Am   **F**   **C**
An innocent man in a living hell.

            F   **C**
That's the story of the Hurricane,

            F
But it won't be over till they clear his name

Dm   **C**   **Dm**
And give him back the time he's done.

          C **Em**   **Am**
Put in a prison cell, but one time he coulda been

F   **C**   **G**
The champion of the world.

D.S. (Instrumental)
          and fade.

You Ain't Goin' Nowhere

Words & Music by Bob Dylan

G   **Am**
Clouds so swift, rain won't lift,

C   **G**
Gate won't close, railings froze.

         Am
Get your mind off wintertime,

C   **G**
You ain't goin' nowhere.

Chorus

G **Am**
Whooee! Ride me high,

  C   **G**
Tomorrow's the day my bride's gonna come.

G   **Am**
Oh, oh, are we gonna fly,

C   **G**
Down in the easy chair!

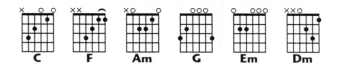

G   **Am**
I don't care, how many letters they sent,

C   **G**
Morning came and morning went.

              Am
Pick up your money and pack up your tent,

C   **G**
You ain't goin' nowhere.

Chorus
G   **Am**
Whooee! Ride me high .....

G   **Am**
Buy me a flute and a gun that shoots

C   **G**
Tailgates and substitutes.

            Am
Strap yourself to the tree with roots,

C   **G**
You ain't goin' nowhere.

Chorus
G   **Am**
Whooee! Ride me high .....

G   **Am**
Genghis Khan he could not keep

C   **G**
All his kings supplied with sleep.

            Am
We'll climb that hill no matter how steep

C   **G**
When we get up to it.

Chorus
G   **Am**
Whooee! Ride me high .....

Blowin' In The Wind

Words & Music by Bob Dylan

C   F   C
How many roads must a man walk down

       F   C   G
Before you call him a man?

      C   F   C
Yes, 'n' how many seas must a white dove sail

       F   G
Before she sleeps in the sand?

      C   F   C
Yes, 'n' how many times must the cannon balls fly

       F   C
Before they're forever banned?

     F   G   C
The answer, my friend, is blowin' in the wind,

     F   G   C
The answer is blowin' in the wind.

C   F   C
How many times must a man look up

       F   C   G
Before he can see the sky?

      C   F   C
Yes, 'n' how many ears must one man have

       F   G
Before he can hear people cry?

      C   F   C
Yes, 'n' how many deaths will it take 'till he knows

       F   C
That too many people have died.

     F   G   C
The answer, my friend, is blowin' in the wind,

     F   G   C
The answer is blowin' in the wind.

C   F   C
How many years can a mountain exist

       F   C   G
Before it's washed to the sea?

      C   F   C
Yes, 'n' how many years can some people exist

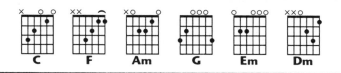

C   F   Am   G   Em   Dm

         F   G
Before they're allowed to be free?

         C   F   C
Yes, 'n' how many times can a man turn his head

            F   C
Pretending he just doesn't see?

     F   G   C
The answer, my friend, is blowin' in the wind,

     F   G   C
The answer is blowin' in the wind.

     F   G   C
The answer is blowin' in the wind.

I And I

Words & Music by Bob Dylan

Dm   **F**   **C**
Been so long since a strange woman has slept in my bed.

G   **Dm**
Look how sweet she sleeps; how free must be her dreams.

               F
In another lifetime she must have owned the world,

     C   **G**
Or been faithfully wed to some righteous king who

                Dm
Wrote psalms beside moonlit streams.

Chorus

Dm   **C**
I and I in creation where one's

    G   **Dm**
Nature neither honors nor forgives.

          C   **G**
I and I. One says to the other,

        Dm
No man sees my face and lives.

Dm   **F**   **C**
Think I'll go out and go for a walk,

G   **Dm**
Not much happenin' here, nothin' ever does.

                  F   **C**
Besides, if she wakes up now, she'll just want me to talk,

G   **Dm**
I got nothin' to say, 'specially about whatever was.

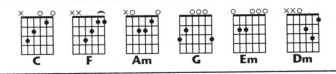

C   F   Am   G   Em   Dm

Chorus

Dm   **C**
    I and I in creation ....

Dm   **F**   **C**
Took an untrodden path once, where the swift don't win the race,
G   **Dm**
It goes to the worthy, who can divide the word of truth.
    F   **C**
Took a stranger to teach me, to look into justice's beautiful face
G   **Dm**
And to see an eye for an eye and a tooth for a tooth.

Chorus

Dm   **C**
    I and I in creation ....

Dm   **F**   **C**
Outside of two men on a train platform there's nobody in sight,
G   **Dm**
They're waiting for spring to come, smoking down the track.
    F   **C**
The world could come to an end tonight, but that's all right,
G   **Dm**
She should still be there sleepin' when I get back.

Chorus

Dm   **C**
    I and I in creation ....

Dm   **F**   **C**
Noontime, and I'm still pushin' myself along the road, the darkest part,
G   **Dm**
Into the narrow lanes, I can't stumble or stay put.
    F   **C**
Someone else is speakin' with my mouth, but I'm listening only to my heart.
G   **Dm**
I've made shoes for everyone, even you, while I still go barefoot.

Chorus

Dm   **C**
    I and I in creation ....

Repeat and fade   **Dm**

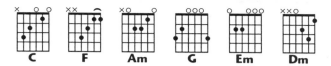

The Ballad Of Frankie Lee And Judas Priest

Words & Music by Bob Dylan

C   **Em**
Well, Frankie Lee and Judas Priest,
Dm   **C**
They were the best of friends,
C   **Em**
So when Frankie Lee needed money one day,
Dm   **C**
Judas quickly pulled out a roll of tens,
           Em
And placed them on a footstool,
    Dm   **C**
Just above the plotted plain,
             Em
Sayin', "Take your pick, Frankie boy,
Dm   **C**
My loss will be your gain."

C   **Em**
Well, Frankie Lee, he sat right down
    Dm   **C**
And put his fingers to his chin,
C   **Em**
But with the cold eyes of Judas on him,
    Dm   **C**
His head began to spin.
    C   **Em**
"Would ya please not stare at me like that," he said,
    Dm   **C**
"It's just my foolish pride,
C   **Em**
But sometimes a man must be alone
    Dm   **C**
And this is no place to hide."

C   **Em**
Well Judas he just winked and said,
    Dm   **C**
"All right I'll leave you here,
C   **Em**
But you'd better hurry up and choose

Which of those bills you want
Dm   **C**
Before they all disappear."
    C   **Em**
"I'm gonna start my pickin' right now,
    Dm   **C**
Just tell me where you'll be."

C   **Em**
Judas pointed down the road
    Dm   **C**
And said, "Eternity!"
C   **Em**
"Eternity?" said Frankie Lee,
    Dm   **C**
With a voice as cold as ice.
  C   **Em**
"That's right," said Judas, "Eternity...
      Dm   **C**
Though you might call it Paradise."

C   **Em**
"I don't call it anything,"
    Dm   **C**
Said Frankie Lee with a smile.
           Em
"All right," said Judas Priest,
Dm   **C**
"I'll see you after a while."

C   **Em**
Well, Frankie Lee, he sat back down,
Dm   **C**
Feelin' low and mean,
             Em
When just then a passing stranger
Dm   **C**
Burst upon the scene,

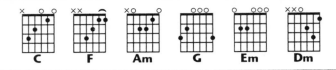

           C   F   Am   G   Em   Dm

                  Em
Saying, "Are you Frankie Lee, the gambler,

Dm   **C**
Whose father is deceased?

Well, if you are,

    Em
There's a fellow callin' you down the road

   Dm   **C**
And they say his name is Priest."

C   **Em**
"Oh yes, he is my friend,"

Dm   **C**
Said Frankie Lee in fright,

    Em
I do recall him very well,

   Dm   **C**
In fact, he just left my sight."

         Em
"Yes, that's the one," said the stranger,

 Dm   **C**
As quiet as a mouse,

C   **Em**
"Well, my message is he's down the road,

Dm   **C**
Stranded in a house."

C   **Em**
Well, Frankie Lee, he panicked,

    Dm   **C**
He dropped ev'rything and ran

     Em
Until he came up to the spot

 Dm   **C**
Where Judas Priest did stand.

     Em
"What kind of house is this," he said,

   Dm   **C**
"Where I have come to roam?"

     Em
"It's not a house," said Judas Priest,

   Dm   **C**
"It's not a house... it's a home."

C   **Em**
Well, Frankie Lee, he trembled,

Dm   **C**
He soon lost all control

        Em
Over ev'rything which he had made

    Dm   **C**
While the mission bells did toll.

         Em
He just stood there staring

      Dm   **C**
At that big house as bright as any sun,

        Em
With four and twenty windows

     Dm   **C**
And a woman's face in ev'ry one.

C   **Em**
Well, up the stairs ran Frankie Lee

    Dm   **C**
With a soulful, bounding leap,

      Em
And, foaming at the mouth,

    Dm   **C**
He began to make his midnight creep.

        Em
For sixteen nights and days he raved,

    Dm   **C**
But on the seventeenth he burst

      Em
Into the arms of Judas Priest,

    Dm   **C**
Which is where he died of thirst.

C   **Em**
No one tried to say a thing

    Dm   **C**
When they took him out in jest,

      Em
Except, of course, the little neighbor boy

    Dm   **C**
Who carried him to rest.

       Em
And he just walked along, alone,

    Dm   **C**
With his guilt so well concealed,

      Em
And muttered underneath his breath,

Dm   **C**
"Nothing is revealed."

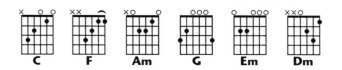

```
 C              Em
```
Well, the moral of the story,
```
     Dm        C
```
The moral of this song,
```
                    Em
```
Is simply that one should never be
```
   Dm                 C
```
Where one does not belong.
```
                          Em
```
So when you see your neighbor carryin' somethin',
```
Dm                      C
```
Help him with his load,
```
                       Em
```
And don't go mistaking Paradise
```
        Dm          C
```
For that home across the road.

Most Of The Time

Words & Music by Bob Dylan

© Copyright 1989 SPECIAL RIDER MUSIC, USA.
This arrangement © Copyright 1991 SPECIAL RIDER MUSIC.
All Rights Reserved. International Copyright Secured.

In verse 4 you can play a simplified version of the E chord (E no 3rd)
by strumming only the lower 3 strings of the Em chord shape,
(leave out the 3rd, 2nd and 1st strings).
When you see the F/G chord symbol, simply play F.
Alternatively, the F/G and E chords are shown at the end of the book,
for you to learn when you feel confident enough to progress.

```
Introduction   C    F
               C       F
```
Most of the time I'm clear focused all around,
```
               C           F
```
Most of the time I can keep both feet on the ground.
```
Am            G F
```
I can follow the path, I can read the signs,
```
Am            G F
```
Stay right with it when the road unwinds,
```
                C           F
```
I can handle whatever I stumble upon.
```
        Am  G    F            C    F C  F
```
I don't even notice she's gone, most of the time.

```
             C F
```
Most of the time it's well understood,
```
             C F
```
Most of the time I wouldn't change it if I could,

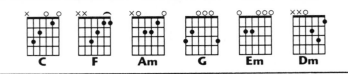

C   **F**   **Am**   **G**   **Em**   **Dm**

Am   **G F**
    I can make it all match up, I can hold my own,

Am   **G F**
    I can deal with the situation right down to the bone.

           C   **F**
    I can survive, I can endure,

             Am G   **F**   **C**   **F**   **C**   **F**
    And I don't even think about her, most of the time.

           C F
    Most of the time my head is on straight,

           C F   **G**
    Most of the time I'm strong enough not to hate.

Am   **G F**   **G**
    I don't build up illusion 'til it makes me sick,

Am   **G F**
    I ain't afraid of confusion no matter how thick.

            C   **F**
    I can smile in the face of mankind,

         Am   **G**   **F**   **C**   **F**   **C**   **F**   **G**
    Don't even remember what her lips felt like on mine, most of the time.

Am   **G C**   **G**
    Most of the time she ain't even in my mind,

Am   **G C**
    I wouldn't know her if I saw her, she's that far behind.

E   **Am**   **E**
    Most of the time I can't even be sure if she was ever with me,

Am   **F**(/G)
    Or if I was ever with her.

          C F
    Most of the time I'm half way content,

          C   **F**   **G**
    Most of the time I know exactly where it went.

Am   **G F**
    I don't cheat on myself, I don't run and hide,

Am   **F**
    Hide from the feelings that are buried inside.

          C   **F**
    I don't compromise and I don't pretend,

        Am   **F**   **C**   **F**
    I don't even care if I ever see her again, most of the time.

Repeat and fade   **C**   **F**

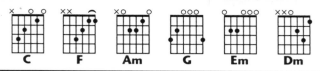

Sara

Words & Music by Bob Dylan

Am
I laid on a dune,

Dm
I looked at the sky,

G
When the children were babies,

Am
And played on the beach.

You came up behind me,

Dm
I saw you go by,

G
You were always so close,

Am
And still within reach.

C Em F
Sara, Sara,

G   **F** **Am**
Whatever made you want to change your mind?

C Em F
Sara, Sara,

G   **F** **Am**
So easy to look at, so hard to define.

Am
I can still see them playin',

Dm
With their pails in the sand,

G
They run to the water,

Am
Their buckets to fill.

I can still see the shells,

Dm
Fallin' out of their hands,

G
As they follow each other,

Am
Back up the hill.

C Em F
Sara, Sara,

G   **F** **Am**
Sweet virgin angel, sweet love of my life.

C Em F
Sara, Sara,

G   **F** **Am**
Radiant jewel, mystical wife.

Am
Sleepin' in the woods,

Dm
By a fire in the night,

G
Drinkin' white rum,

Am
In a Portugal bar.

Them playin' leap-frog,

Dm
And hearin' about Snow White,

G
You in the market place,

Am
In Savanna-la-Mar.

C Em F
Sara, Sara,

G   **F** **Am**
It's all so clear, I could never forget.

C Em F
Sara, Sara,

G   **F** **Am**
Lovin' you is the one thing I'll never regret.

Am
I can still hear the sounds,

Dm
Of those Methodist bells,

G
I'd taken the cure,

Am
And had just gotten through

Stayin' up for days,

Dm
In the Chelsea Hotel,

G
Writin' "Sad-Eyed Lady

Am
Of the Lowlands" for you.

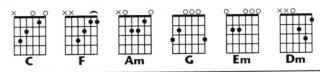

C Em F
Sara, Sara,

    G   **F**   **Am**
Wherever we travel we're never apart.

C Em F
Sara, oh Sara,

G   **F**   **Am**
Beautiful lady, so dear to my heart.

Am
How did I meet you,

Dm
I don't know,

  G
A messenger sent me,

  Am
In a tropical storm.

You were there in the winter,

    Dm
Moonlight on the snow,

    G
And on Lily Pond Lane,

    Am
When the weather was warm.

C Em F
Sara, oh Sara,

G   **F**   **Am**
Scorpio Sphinx in a calico dress.

C Em F
Sara, Sara,

  G   **F**   **Am**
You must forgive me my unworthiness.

        Am
Now the beach is deserted,

    Dm
Except for some kelp,

      G
And a piece of old ship,

      Am
That lies on the shore.

You always responded,

      Dm
When I needed your help,

  G
You gimme a map,

      Am
And a key to your door.

C Em F
Sara, oh Sara,

G   **F**   **Am**
Glamorous nymph with an arrow and bow.

C Em F
Sara, oh Sara,

G   **F**   **Am**
Don't ever leave me, don't ever go.

John Wesley Harding

Words & Music by Bob Dylan
© *Copyright 1968, 1976 DWARF MUSIC, USA.*
This arrangement © Copyright 1991 DWARF MUSIC.
All Rights Reserved. International Copyright Secured.

Wherever you see the chord symbol G7 you may play the G chord.
Alternatively you may want to learn The G7 chord which is shown at the end of the book.

C   **F** **G** **C**
John Wesley Harding was a friend to the poor,

                  Dm **F** **G**
He trav'led with a gun in ev'ry hand.

C   **F**   **G**   **C**
All along this countryside, he opened a many a door,

                F   **G**(7) **C**
But he was never known to hurt an honest man.

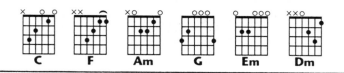

      C   **F**   **G**   **C**
'Twas down in Chaynee County, a time they talk about,

                                 Dm **F** **G**
With his lady by his side he took a stand.

      C   **F**   **G**   **C**
And soon the situation there was all but straightened out,

                        F   **G**(7) **C**
For he was always known to lend a helping hand.

    C   **F**   **G**   **C**
All across the telegraph his name it did resound,

                             Dm **F** **G**
But no charge held against him could they prove.

          C   **F**   **G**   **C**
And there was no man around who could track or chain him down,

               F   **G**(7) **C**
He was never known to make a foolish move.

Most Likely You Go Your Way

Words & Music by Bob Dylan

Wherever you see the C7 chord symbol, you may play the C chord.
Alternatively you may want to learn the C7 chord which is shown at the end of the book.

Dm
You say you love me and you're thinkin' of me,

                        C(7)
But you know you could be wrong.

Dm
You say you told me that you wanna hold me,

                        C
But you know you're not that strong.

Em   **Am**
I just can't do what I done before,

Dm
I just can't beg you any more,

        C   **C**(7) **G**
I'm gonna let you pass and I'll go last.

        C   **Em** **F**   **C**
Then time will tell just who fell,

      F   **G**
And who's been left behind,

                    C(7)
When you go your way and I go mine.

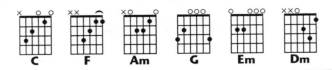

C   **F**   **Am**   **G**   **Em**   **Dm**

Dm
   You say you disturb me and you don't deserve me,

                        C(7)
But you know sometimes you lie.

Dm
   You say you're shakin' and you're always achin',

                        C(7)
But you know how hard you try.

Em   **Am**
Sometimes it gets so hard to care,

Dm
   It can't be this way ev'rywhere.

              C   **C**(7)   **G**
And I'm gonna let you pass, yes and I'll go last.

          C   **Em** **F**   **C**
Then, time will tell just who fell,

       F   **G**
And who's been left behind,

                   C(7)
When you go your way and I go mine.

Am
   The judge, he holds a grudge,

           G
He's gonna call on you,

          Am
But he's badly built and he walks on stilts,

           G
Watch out he don't fall on you.

Dm
   You say you're sorry for tellin' stories

                   C(7)
That you know I believe are true.

Dm
   You say you got some other kind of lover,

              C(7)
And yes I believe you do.

Em
   You say my kisses are not like his,

          Dm
But this time I'm not gonna tell you why that is.

          C   **G**
I'm just gonna let you pass, yes and I'll go last

       C   **Em** **F**   **C**
Then, time will tell who fell,

       F   **G**
And who's been left behind,

                   C(7)
When you go your way and I go mine.

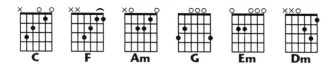

C   F   Am   G   Em   Dm

Isis

Music by Bob Dylan
Words by Bob Dylan & Jacques Levy

G   F   C   G
I married Isis on the fifth day of May,
              F   C   G
But I could not hold on to her very long.
         F   C   G
So I cut off my hair and I rode straight away,
             F   C   G
For the wild unknown country where I could not go wrong.

G   F   C   G
I came to a high place of darkness and light.
         F   C   G
The dividing line ran through the center of town.
         F   C   G
I hitched up my pony to a post on the right.
         F   C   G
Went into a laundry to wash my clothes down.

G   F   C   G
A man in the corner approached me for a match.
         F   C   G
I knew right away he was not ordinary.
         F   C   G
He said, "Are you lookin' for somethin' easy to catch?"
         F   C   G
I said, "I got no money." He said, "That ain't necessary."

G   F   C   G
We set out that night for the cold in the North.
         F   C   G
I gave him my blanket, he gave me his word.
         F   C   G
I said, "Where are we goin'?" He said we'd be back by the fourth.
         F   C G
I said, "That's the best news that I've ever heard."

G   F   C   G
I was thinkin' about turquoise, I was thinkin' about gold,
         F   C   G
I was thinkin' about diamonds and the world's biggest necklace.

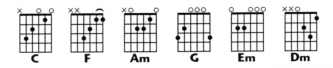

        F   **C** **G**
As we rode through the canyons, through the devilish cold,
        F   **C**   **G**
I was thinkin' about Isis, how she thought I was so reckless.

  G   **F**   **C** **G**
How she told me that one day we would meet up again,
      F   **C**   **G**
And things would be different the next time we wed,
    F   **C**   **G**
If I could only hang on and just be her friend.
      F   **C**   **G**
I still can't remember all the best things she said.

  G   **F**   **C**   **G**
We came to the pyramids all embedded in ice.
     F   **C** **G**
He said, "There's a body I'm tryin' to find,
     F   **C**   **G**
If I carry it out it'll bring a good price."
     F   **C**   **G**
'Twas then that I knew what he had on his mind.

  G   **F**   **C**   **G**
The wind it was howlin' and the snow was outrageous.
      F   **C**   **G**
We chopped through the night and we chopped through the dawn.
      F   **C**   **G**
When he died I was hopin' that it wasn't contagious,
      F   **C**   **G**
But I made up my mind that I had to go on.

  G   **F** **C**   **G**
I broke into the tomb, but the casket was empty.
      F   **C**   **G**
There was no jewels, no nothin', I felt I'd been had.
      F   **C** **G**
When I saw that my partner was just bein' friendly,
      F **C**   **G**
When I took up his offer I must-a been mad.

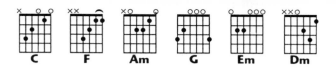

C   F   Am   G   Em   Dm

G   F   C   G
I picked up his body and I dragged him inside,

                    F   C   G
Threw him down in the hole and I put back the cover.

               F   C   G
I said a quick prayer and I felt satisfied.

                 F   C   G
Then I rode back to find Isis just to tell her I love her.

        G   F   C   G
She was there in the meadow where the creek used to rise.

           F   C   G
Blinded by sleep and in need of a bed,

           F   C   G
I came in from the East with the sun in my eyes.

           F   C   G
I cursed her one time then I rode on ahead.

      G   F   C   G
She said, "Where ya been?" I said, "No place special."

               F   C   G
She said, "You look different." I said, "Well, not quite."

               F   C   G
She said, "You been gone." I said, "That's only natural."

               F   C G
She said, "You gonna stay?" I said, "yeah, I jes might."

G   F   C   G
Isis, oh Isis, you mystical child.

           F   C   G
What drives me to you is what drives me insane.

           F   C   G
I still can remember the way that you smiled

           F   C   G
On the fifth day of May in the drizzlin' rain.

Chord diagrams: C, F, Am, G, Em, Dm

If Not For You

Words & Music by Bob Dylan

*Wherever you see Dm7 you may play Dm. Wherever you see the chord symbol D
you may play a simplified version of the chord (D no 3rd) by strumming the
D minor shape from the 4th string to the 2nd string only (leave out the 1st string).
The Dm7 and D chords are shown at the end of the book.*

```
         C F        C        F
If not for you, Babe, I couldn't find the door,

          C      F
Couldn't even see the floor,

          Em
I'd be sad and blue,

Dm(7)       C   F   C   F
If not for you.
```

```
F        C F          C
If not for you, Babe, I'd lay awake all night,

F        C        F       Em
Wait for the mornin' light to shine in through,

Dm(7)        Em
But it would not be new,

Dm(7)       C   F   C   F
If not for you.
```

Chorus

```
F          C
If not for you my sky would fall,

G            C
Rain would gather too.

F             C
Without your love I'd be nowhere at all,

D          G       F       Em   Dm(7)   C
I'd be lost if not for you, and you know it's true.
```

```
F          C
If not for you my sky would fall,

G            C
Rain would gather too.

F             C
Without your love I'd be nowhere at all,

D          G    F    Em   Dm(7)   C
Oh! what would I do, if not for you.
```

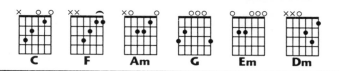

C   **F**   **Am**   **G**   **Em**   **Dm**

      F   **C**
If not for you, winter would have no spring,

F   **C**   **F**   **Em**
Couldn't hear the robin sing, I just wouldn't have a clue,

Dm(7)   **Em**
Anyway it wouldn't ring true,

Dm(7)   **C F**   **C**
If not for you. If not for you.

Repeat and fade

F   **C**
If not for you.

I Shall be Released

Words & Music by Bob Dylan & Richard Manuel

Wherever you see the chord symbol G7 you may play the G chord.
The G7 chord is shown at the end of the book.

C   **Dm**
They say ev'rything can be replaced,

Em   **Dm**   **C**   **G**(7)
Yet ev'ry distance is not near.

C   **Dm**
So I remember ev'ry face,

Em   **Dm**   **C**   **G**(7)
Of ev'ry man who put me here.

Chorus

C   **Dm**
I see my light come shining,

Em   **Dm**   **C**   **G**(7)
From the west unto the east.

C   **Dm**
Any day now, any day now,

Em Dm   **C**
I shall be released.

C   **Dm**
They say ev'ry man needs protection,

Em   **Dm**   **C**   **G**(7)
They say ev'ry man must fall.

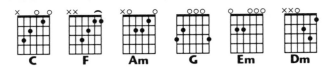

C Yet I swear I see my **Dm** reflection,

Em Some place so **Dm** high above this **C** wall. **G**(7)

Chorus

C I see my light come **Dm** ....

C Standing next to me in this lonely **Dm** crowd,

Em Is a man who **Dm** swears he's not to **C** blame. **G**(7)

C All day long I hear him shout so **Dm** loud,

Em Crying out **Dm** that he was **C** framed. **G**(7)

Chorus

C I see my light come **Dm** ....

I Pity The Poor Immigrant

Words & Music by Bob Dylan
© *Copyright 1968, 1976 DWARF MUSIC, USA.*
This arrangement © Copyright 1991 DWARF MUSIC.
All Rights Reserved. International Copyright Secured.

Wherever you see the G7 chord symbol, you may play the G chord.
Alternatively, you can learn the G7 chord which is shown at the end of the book.

C **F**
I pity the poor immigrant,

G(7) **C**
Who wishes he would've stayed home.

F
Who uses all his power to do evil,

G(7) **C**
But in the end is always left so alone.

Am **Em**
That man who with his fingers cheats,

F **C**
And who lies with ev'ry breath.

F
Who passionately hates his life,

G(7) **C**
And likewise, fears his death.

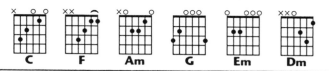

C   F
I pity the poor immigrant,

    G(7)   C
Whose strength is spent in vain.

         C   F
Whose heaven is like Ironsides,

    G(7)   C
Whose tears are like rain.

     Am   Em
Who eats but is not satisfied,

    F   C
Who hears but does not see.

    C   F
Who falls in love with wealth itself,

    G(7)   C
And turns his back on me.

   C   F
I pity the poor immigrant,

    G(7)   C
Who tramples through the mud,

    C   F
Who fills his mouth with laughing,

    G(7)   C
And who builds his town with blood.

     Am   Em
Whose visions in the final end,

    F   C
Must shatter like the glass.

   C   F
I pity the poor immigrant,

    G(7)   C
When his gladness comes to pass.

What Good Am I?

Words & Music by Bob Dylan

When you see the F/C chord you may play F.
Alternatively the F/C chord is shown at the end of the book.

C   F   C   F(/c) C
   What good am I if I'm like all the rest.

                  F   C
If I just turn away when I see how you're dressed,

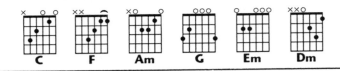

C **F** **Am** **G** **Em** **Dm**

Am   **Em**
If I shut myself off so I can't hear you cry,

F   **C**   **F C**   **F***(/c)* **C**
What good am I?

F*(/c)*   **C** **F**   **C**   **F C**
What good am I if I know and don't do,

                F   **C**   **F C**
If I see and don't say, if I look right through you,

     Am   **Em**
If I turn a deaf ear to the thunderin' sky,

F   **C**   **F C**   **F C**
What good am I?

             F   **C**   **F C**
What good am I while you softly weep,

                 F   **C**   **F C**
And I hear in my head what you say in your sleep,

     Am   **Em**
And I freeze in the moment like the rest who don't try,

F   **C**   **F C**   **F C**
What good am I?

     Am
What good am I then to others and me,

                 Em
If I've had every chance and yet still fail to see,

     Am
If my hands are tied, must I not wonder within,

          Em   **Dm**
Who tied them and why and where must I have been?

C   **F**   **C**   **F C**
What good am I if I say foolish things,

            F   **C**   **F C**
And I laugh in the face of what sorrow brings,

     Am   **Em**
And I just turn my back while you silently die,

F   **C** **F C**   **F C**   **F C**
What good am I?

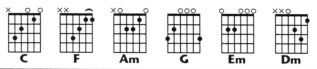

Forever Young

Words & Music by Bob Dylan

Wherever you see the chord symbol G7 or G7 sus 4 you may play the G chord.
The G7 & G7 sus 4 chords are shown at the end of the book.

    C
May God bless and keep you always,

    F   **C**
May your wishes all come true.

May you always do for others,

    G(7)
And let others do for you.

    C
May you build a ladder to the stars,

 F
And climb on every rung.

    C **G**(7) **G**(7 sus 4) **C**   **F**
May you stay forever   young,

    G(7)   **C**
Forever young, forever young

    C **G**(7) **G**(7 sus 4) **C**
May you stay forever   young.

Instrumental

C   **F** **C**   **G**(7)   **C** **F**   **C** **G**(7) **C** **F** **C** **G**(7) **C**

    C
May you grow up to be righteous,

    F   **C**
May you grow up to be true.

    C
May you always know the truth,

    G(7)
And see the lights surrounding you.

    C
May you always be courageous,

   F
Stand upright and be strong.

    C **G**(7) **G**(7 sus 4) **C**   **F**
May you stay forever   young,

    G(7)   **C**
Forever young, forever young

    C **G**(7) **G**(7 sus 4) **C**
May you stay forever   young.

Instrumental

C   **F** **C**   **G**(7)   **C** **F**   **C** **G**(7) **C** **F** **C** **G**(7) **C**

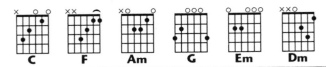

C   C
May your hands always be busy,

    F   C
May your feet always be swift.

May you have a strong foundation,

     G(7)
When the winds of changes shift.

     C
May your heart always be joyful,

    F
May your song always be sung.

     C G(7) G(7 sus 4) C   F
May you stay forever   young,

   G(7)   C
Forever young, forever young.

     C G(7) G(7 sus 4) C
May you stay forever   young.

Instrumental

C F C   G(7)   C F C G(7) C F C G(7) C

Stuck Inside Of Mobile With The Memphis Blues Again

Words & Music by Bob Dylan

Wherever you see the G7 chord symbol you may play the G chord.
Alternatively, you can learn the G7 chord which is shown at the end of the book.

   C   Am
Oh, the ragman draws circles,

C   Am
Up and down the block.

  C   Am
I'd ask him what the matter was,

   F   G(7)
But I know that he don't talk.

    F   C
And the ladies treat me kindly,

Am   C
And furnish me with tape.

Am   C
But deep inside my heart,

F   C
I know I can't escape.

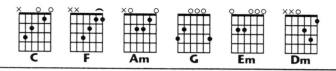

C   F   Am   G   Em   Dm

Chorus

Em C   **Em**   **F**
Oh, mama, can this really be the end,

C   **Em   Am**   **C**
To be stuck inside of Mobile with the

F
Memphis blues again.   **G**(7)

C   **Am**
Well, Shakespeare, he's in the alley,

C   **Am**
With his pointed shoes and his bells.

C   **Am**
Speaking to some French girl,

F   **G**(7)
Who says she knows me well.

F   **C**
And I would send a message,

Am   **C**
To find out if she's talked.

Am   **C**
But the post office has been stolen,

F   **C**
And the mail box is locked.

Chorus

Em C   **Em**
Oh, mama, can this really ....

C   **Am**
Mona tried to tell me,

C   **Am**
To stay away from the train line.

C   **Am**
She said that all the railroad men,

F   **G**(7)
Just drink up your blood like wine.

F   **C**
An' I said, "Oh, I didn't know that,

Am   **C**
But then, again, there's only one I've met,

Am   **C**
An' he just smoked my eyelids,

F   **C**
An' punched my cigarette."

Chorus

Em C   **Em**
Oh, mama, can this really ....

C   **Am**
Grandpa died last week,

C   **Am**
And now he's buried in the rocks.

C   **Am**
But every one still talks about,

F   **G**(7)
How badly they were shocked.

F   **C**
But me, I expected it to happen,

Am   **C**
I knew he'd lost control.

Am   **C**
When he built a fire on Main Street,

F   **C**
And shot it full of holes.

Chorus

Em C   **Em**
Oh, mama, can this really ....

C   **Am**
Now the senator came down here,

C   **Am**
Showing ev'ryone his gun.

C   **Am**
Handing out free tickets,

F   **G**(7)
To the wedding of his son.

F   **C**
An' me, I nearly got busted,

Am   **C**
An' wouldn't it be my luck

Am   **C**
To get caught without a ticket,

F   **C**
And be discovered beneath a truck.

Chorus

Em C   **Em**
Oh, mama, can this really ....

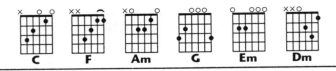

C   F   Am   G   Em   Dm

C   Am
Now the preacher looked so baffled,

C   Am
When I asked him why he dressed

C   Am
With twenty pounds of headlines,

F   G(7)
Stapled to his chest.

F   C
But he cursed me when I proved it to him,

Am   C
Then I whispered, "Not even you can hide,

Am   C
You see, you're just like me.

F   C
I hope you're satisfied."

Chorus

Em C   Em
Oh, mama, can this really ....

C   Am
Now the rainman gave me two cures,

C   Am
Then he said, "Jump right in."

C   Am
The one was Texas medicine,

F   G(7)
The other was just railroad gin.

F   C
An' like a fool I mixed them,

Am   C
An' it strangled up my mind.

Am   C
An' now people just get uglier,

F   C
An' I have no sense of time.

Chorus

Em C   Em
Oh, mama, can this really ....

C   Am
When Ruthie says come see her,

C   Am
In her honky-tonk lagoon.

C   Am
Where I can watch her waltz for free,

F   G(7)
'Neath her Panamanian moon.

F   C
An' I say, "Aw come on now,

Am   C
You must know about my debutante."

Am   Am
An' she says, "Your debutante just knows

C
what you need,

F   C
But I know what you want."

Chorus

Em C   Em
Oh, mama, can this really ....

C   Am
Now the bricks lay on Grand Street,

C   Am
Where the neon madmen climb.

C   Am
They all fall there so perfectly,

F   G(7)
It all seems so well timed.

F   C
And here I sit so patiently,

Am   C
Waiting to find out what price

Am   C
You have to pay to get out of

F   C
Going thru all these things twice.

Chorus

Em C   Em
Oh, mama, can this really ....

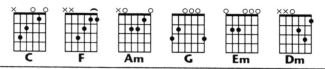

Is Your Love In Vain?

Words & Music by Bob Dylan

Wherever you see the chord symbol G/B, you may play the G chord.
Where you see the chord symbol C/G, you may play the C chord.
Alternatively, turn to the end of the book to learn of an easy way to play
the G/B chord and see the C/G chord.

   C **G**(/B) **Am** **C**
Do you love me,

    F   **G**
Or are you just extending goodwill?

   C   **G**(/B) **Am** **C**(/G)
Do you need me half as bad as you say,

    F   **G**
Or are you just feeling guilt?

   Am   **C**(/G) **F**   **C**
I've been burned before and I know the score,

    F   **G**
So you won't hear me complain.

C   **G**(/B) **Am** **C**(/G)
Will I be able to count on you,

  F   **G**   **C**
Or is your love in vain?

   C   **G**(/B)   **Am** **C**
Are you so fast that you cannot see

    F   **G**
That I must have solitude?

   C **G**(/B) **Am** **C**(/G)
When I am in the darkness,

F   **G**
Why do you intrude.

   Am   **C**(/G)   **F**   **C**
Do you know my world, do you know my kind

F   **G**
Or must I explain?

C   **G**(/B) **Am** **C**(/G)
Will you let me be myself,

  F   **G**   **C**
Or is your love in vain?

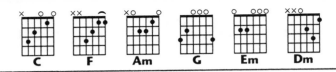

<pre>
     F   G   C   Am
Well, I've been to the mountain and I've been in the wind,

     F   G C
I've been in and out of happiness.

     F   G   C   Am
I have dined with kings, I've been offered wings,

     F   G
And I've never been too impressed.

  C G(/B)   Am   C
Alright, I'll take a chance,

        F   G
I will fall in love with you.

   C   G(/B)   Am   C(/G)
If I'm a fool , you can have the night

        F   G
You can have the morning too.

     Am   C(/G)   F   C
Can you cook and sew, make flowers grow,

        F   G
Do you understand my pain?

C   G(/B)   Am   C(/G)
Are you willing to risk it all,

     F   G   C   G(/B) Am   C(/G)   F   G   C
Or is your love in vain?
</pre>

Chord Glossary

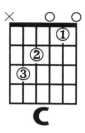

C

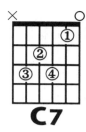

C7

C sus 4

Easy To Play

C sus 4

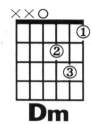

Dm

Dm7

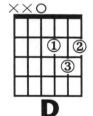

D

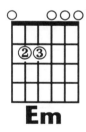

Em

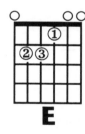

E

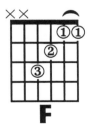

F

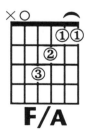

F/A

F/G

Chord Glossary

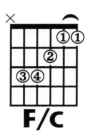

F/C

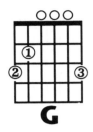

G

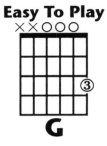

G

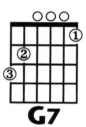

G7

Easy To Play

G7

G/B

G7sus4

Easy To Play

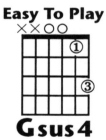

Gsus4

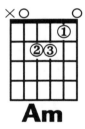

Am

10/97(29095)

Arnos Vale Bristol

A VICTORIAN CEMETERY

Friends of Arnos Vale Cemetery

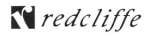

We think we may in all safety predict, when all arrangements are completed, the grounds planted, the various tombs and memorials erected, that few if any cemeteries in the kingdom will surpass the Cemetery at Arnos Vale.

Felix Farley's Bristol Journal, October 1840

First published in 2007 by Redcliffe Press Ltd.,
81g Pembroke Road, Bristol BS8 3EA
www.redcliffepress.co.uk
info@redcliffepress.co.uk

ISBN 978-1-904537-76-2
British Library Cataloguing-in-Publication Data
A catalogue record for this book is available from the British Library

Design, typesetting and contributory photography by Stephen Morris smc@freeuk.com www.stephen-morris.co.uk
Printed by HSW Print, Tonypandy, Rhondda

Arnos Vale Bristol

DEDICATION

THIS BOOK IS PUBLISHED BY THE FRIENDS OF ARNOS VALE CEMETERY and is drawn from the many years of research by a number of people committed to the preservation and restoration of Arnos Vale, Bristol. It is not a guide book but simply the story of the long and chequered history of one of Bristol's hidden and nearly lost treasures. It is not a quick dash through 45 Victorian acres, noting a brief inscription here and there, but a carefully researched work written with love – a tale to be savoured through a warm summer evening or at a cosy winter fireside.

It is dedicated to the memory of Les Owen, who generously made his lifetime's research freely available, and also to members of the Friends and others, who are not mentioned on these pages but know they are part of them.

Oh let me lie in a quiet spot, with the green turf o'er my head,
Far from the city's busy hum, the worldling's heavy tread;
Where the free winds blow, and the branches wave,
And the songbirds sweetly sing,
Till every mourner here exclaims, 'O Death, where is thy sting?'
Where, in nothing that blooms around, about, the living e'er can see
That grave that covers my earthly frame has won a victory;
Where bright flowers bloom through the summer-time, to tell how all was given
To fade away from the eyes of men and live again in heaven.

Mary Carpenter: 1807-1877
Bristol social reformer buried at Arnos Vale

PROLOGUE

ON THE BATH ROAD IN BRISTOL, AMIDST ALL TOO GRIMLY TYPICAL
twentieth-century development, there stands a nineteenth-century
Elysian enclave, a great tract of Victorian planting at its most
picturesque; an arboretum, a botanic garden and a nature reserve; a
landscape that sets off to perfection the architectural utopia in
miniature before you with classical temples and columns, domes,
canopies and obelisks, gothic pinnacles and gables, as well as an
Indian temple, all presenting a showpiece of the architect's,
sculptor's, stonemason's and letterer's art.

Arnos Vale might well be one of the most important cemeteries in
the British Isles. I have delighted in hundreds and can with
confidence say that in terms of topography, planting, memorial design
and, above all, excellence of architecture, Arnos Vale would be hard
to beat.

Arnos Vale has been a great discovery to me. I now realise the full
extent of its importance and that of the host of heroes buried there;
yet there would have been no hope for Arnos Vale if it were not for
the local people, the Trustees and Friends of Arnos Vale who continue
to work so hard to preserve and restore the site.

By buying this book, you are also helping the campaign. Thank you.

Lucinda Lambton
Patron of Arnos Vale Cemetery Trust

INTRODUCTION

LOCATED BETWEEN THE A4 AND THE A37 IN BRISTOL, ARNOS VALE IS A HIDDEN TREASURE, A secret garden behind Victorian gateways. It stands as an oasis of peace and rest in an urban desert, and to the first-time visitor it offers a landscape of breathtaking beauty in all seasons. It contains 50,000 graves, and yet Arnos Vale is a garden cemetery brimming with life. Perhaps because of its design, or perhaps because it came so close to being lost forever, it offers each visitor a personal welcome.

By the early 1980s, Arnos Vale was in crisis. There was no more land available for burials, and pathways had become narrow, overgrown and sinister. Notices appeared, encouraging visitors to consider exhumation of their loved ones to alternative locations. Where once the visitor had lingered in the sunshine on pleasant benches, many areas had become dark and unwelcoming to the few brave souls who continued to visit their family graves. The crematorium, set up to supplement the dwindling income in the 1920s, now faced serious competition from new and efficient installations in the same area. The whole Cemetery was in decline.

Serene stone angels and celtic crosses rose above graves overgrown with bramble; birds nested and butterflies thrived amongst the trees and shrubs, and ivy and bindweed crept over the inscriptions to people who were once so loved but now forgotten, wrapping the older graves in a protective green mantle. Elegant and graceful listed buildings and ornate monuments stood proud in an urban wilderness.

Nature has her own method of dealing with man's dereliction and now Arnos Vale is a haven for wildlife. Hardly any chemical fertilisers or weedkillers have been used on the site, giving plants and animals the chance to thrive in a largely uncontaminated environment. It has been designated a Site of Nature Conservation Interest, such is its natural significance. Sunlight dapples the little paths which meander off into the woodlands. In spring, these same pathways are smothered with primroses, and in summer the butterflies and insects dance in their secret bluebell glades and quiet, remote spots. In autumn, spider webs glisten in the dawn light against a backdrop of the jewelled tints of the trees. And in winter the low sunlight, shafting between the graves, casts shadows and illuminates the faces of the angels and cherubs, giving Arnos Vale a distinctive beauty all of its own. After snowfall, the whole landscape is transformed into a silent ethereal scene of twinkling diamonds and arctic peaks, suggesting a rare glimpse of a paradise once so nearly lost.

Arnos Vale is still a working cemetery and many people visit to remember and feel close to their loved ones – a last point of contact – to tidy graves, to walk and think and be at peace in the tranquillity.

The 50,000 graves in the 45 acres of Arnos Vale contain the mortal remains of 170,000 people who lived in and around the City of Bristol and helped to fashion its future. In addition, over 120,000 cremations took place there, with cremated remains being scattered in the Gardens of Rest or interred elsewhere in the Cemetery. It would be totally unrealistic to believe that all those graves and gardens would be visited by descendants down the ages and never forgotten. In *Middlemarch*, George Eliot wrote:

> … the growing good of the world is partly dependent on unhistoric acts; and that things are not so ill with you and me as they might have been, is half owing to the number who lived faithfully a hidden life, and rest in unvisited tombs.

These pages remember and honour those whose last resting place is Arnos Vale; not only the celebrities, social reformers, nautical and military heroes, campaigners, religious pioneers and successful business people, but also the thousands of ordinary people – a 19-year-old who died trying to rescue a child from the river, a policeman murdered when he stepped in to protect a donkey being savagely beaten by its owner, the railway workers, the family servants, the heart-breakingly high numbers of Victorian children who died in infancy, the destitute and unloved, the orphans and those who loved and cared for them, and the victims of two world wars.

Arnos Vale provides us with lasting information about how people lived their lives and how attitudes to life and death have changed over time. For historians and those researching their family history, the monuments and inscriptions are invaluable and unique.

And then there is the architecture. Arnos Vale boasts four impressive Grade II* listed buildings, two Grade II* listed tombs, and over twenty Grade II listed tombs. The two gate lodges at the Bath Road entrance and the two mortuary chapels are superb examples of Victorian design and craftsmanship at its very best. In addition, the lower Arcadian Garden area is included on the Register of Historic Parks and Gardens.

This book has been produced by the Friends of Arnos Vale Cemetery. They hope you will enjoy reading it, that you will find it helpful and informative, and above all that it will inspire you to visit. But be warned, one visit is never enough.

ARNOS VALE BRISTOL. 463

THE EARLY DAYS

It is likely that the site of Arnos Vale has been occupied in some form since before Roman times. The remains of a Roman villa, which may have been part of a large estate, have been found in Brislington.

The Domesday Book records 'Brisilton' as part of the manor of 'Cainesham' or Keynsham, and the chequered history of the land now occupied by Arnos Vale Cemetery can be traced back almost a thousand years.

In 1087, William II, who was known as 'Rufus' because of his red hair, made 'Brisilton' a manor in its own right when he deeded the land to William Fitz-Hammond, a nephew of William the Conqueror. He in turn gave the estate to Robert, Earl of Gloucester, when Robert married Fitz-Hammond's daughter, Mabel. Efforts to keep the land in the family continued for a further generation. Robert's son, William of Gloucester, made John (the son of Henry II) his heir. John later married William's sister, Isabelle. John, however, gave the estate to the de la Warr family for 'services rendered to the Crown'.

The de la Warrs (who gave their name to the USA state of Delaware) were a hugely influential family, who ruled the manor from the late 1100s to the late 1500s. They built a moated manor house on the site which is now West Town Lane.

The land now occupied by Arnos Vale Cemetery passed to Thomas Lacy in 1640, and was purchased by Thomas Langton in 1653. Links with the Langton family and the Langton Court Estate still remain in local road names and inscriptions on headstones. By 1660 the site had become a smallholding owned by the Newton family.

In the 1700s, Brislington was a fashionable retreat for Bristol's wealthy merchants. At that time, it was still completely rural, removed from the hustle, bustle, sounds and smells of the rapidly expanding city, yet close enough for the merchants to be able to keep an eye on their investments. Some built grand houses and moved their families out of the city. Others would ride out for social occasions and for leisure activities.

In 1760 the property had passed into the hands of William Reeve, a wealthy Quaker copper smelter. He was a maternal grandson of the Newtons who had married into the prosperous Harford dynasty. The Harfords, also Quakers (usually known as the Religious Society of Friends), owned a number of copper smelting works and brass foundries situated along the banks of the river Avon and lived in quiet dignity on the Hanham side of the river. Reeve began acquiring land adjacent to his own and commissioned the building of a splendid house at Arnos Court, which in later years became a convent and girls reformatory school, and is now an hotel.

The Black Castle, today a restaurant on the opposite side of the A4 Bath Road, was Reeve's stable block and also provided accommodation for his servants and a private chapel. The smelters had found themselves in trouble with the City Council over the disposal of smelting waste, which they used to dump on the river banks hoping that the tides would wash it away. The Black Castle was built with bricks made from the waste of the copper smelting process and is one of the best surviving examples of early recycling. Its nickname in those days was less flattering for it was known locally as 'The Devil's Cathedral'.

Reeve offended his in-laws in a major way and, in 1774, they bankrupted him and he was expelled from the Society of Friends. There seems to be no record of his misdemeanours but the Harford family stated: '… it appears that the conduct of William Reeve hath been reproachful and inconsistent with our religious principles…' Somewhat high-handed, perhaps, considering that the Harfords were producing and exporting copper and brass wares, some of which would have almost certainly been used on the sugar plantations of the West Indies when slavery was at its height.

The land owned by Reeve was broken up into smaller parcels and sold off at favourable prices. The Arnos Vale Cemetery site was bought by John Cave, banker to the Harford family. A direct line from John Cave leads to the NatWest Bank. His sons built a manor house at Downend where their tythe cottages, called Cave Cottages, still stand. A new road, Cave Close, has also been named after the family.

John Cave built himself a comfortable house where Soldiers' Corner (the World War I memorial) now stands, and he lived out the rest of his life there. The house was later sold to the sugar refiner, Philip Worsley. When the site came onto the open market for sale in the 1830s, there had been plans to build the new Bristol Zoo there. However, the zoo was finally located in Clifton and the newly-formed Bristol General Cemetery Company chose the Brislington site for their cemetery. Cave's house was demolished.

RIVERS and CHOLERA

Until the start of the nineteenth century, the river Avon was tidal so each day the raw sewage and other unimaginable debris that went into the Avon, either directly from the city streets or from the river Frome which flowed into it, would be flushed out through the Avon Gorge and into the Severn Estuary.

By the early 1800s, this cleansing tidal flow was causing problems for the Bristol City Docks Committee. The harbour was of immense importance to the city's merchants and businessmen, but ships were getting bigger all the time and when the tide was out they were in danger of keeling over on the mud and suffering severe damage.

Only vessels so well built that they could withstand the strains of the tidal system, and so well ordered that everything was firmly tied down to prevent accidents when the ship lurched on the mud at the bottom of the river, were deemed to be 'ship-shape and Bristol fashion'. As most ships came nowhere near this standard, business suffered.

It was decided to dam the river near Temple Meads via a series of locks, and provide a permanent 'floating harbour' which would allow ships to remain at high water level and avoid the damage caused by the effects of the 30-ft tides ebbing and flowing. The river Avon, meanwhile, was diverted through the New Cut Canal which took the excess water from the weir at Netham Lock, around the city, and out to Hotwells.

The engineer William Jessop masterminded this incredible work. The Feeder Canal was built between Netham Lock and Temple Meads to supply the water necessary to maintain a constant level in the harbour – hence its name. Entrance locks and basins were also built.

The work was completed in 1809 at a cost of £600,000, about twice the original estimate, and there were great celebrations. A feast was provided for the thousand men who had worked on the project, literally moving thousands of tons of earth by hand. The party started off well with the labourers tucking into two oxen, roasted whole, a proportionate weight of potatoes, six hundredweight of plum pudding and a gallon of strong beer or 'stingo' per guest. The stingo was possibly a mistake because a fight broke out and the press gang had to be called in to suppress the fracas.

So why was the completion of the New Cut and the Floating Harbour relevant to Arnos Vale? Unfortunately this great scheme was almost certainly responsible for some of the city's

The Quay at St Augustine's Back

subsequent public health problems. Although the appearance of the city centre had been greatly improved, the fact remained that ever-increasing amounts of raw sewage were still going directly into the rivers Frome and Avon. But instead of being washed away by the higher tides, the effluent was now being trapped in the new docks in a relatively small area of water in the centre of the most populous part of the city. The waste could only escape on the occasions when the lock gates were opened.

It is difficult today to imagine the conditions that existed in Bristol at the beginning of the nineteenth century. The central area around the rivers Avon and Frome was a warren of narrow streets. Each house discharged its sewage and other waste into the street and each street then discharged directly into the open waters of the rivers and the harbour. The larger houses of the more prosperous citizens relied on privies and cesspits. Those with riverside houses usually sited their privies on an upper floor overhanging the riverbanks, hoping that the higher tides would wash away the sewage.

The water supplies came from the old monastic pipe system or from wells, many of which were situated inside churchyards which, of course, were also cemeteries. Some people earned their living from selling 'clean' water but it was very expensive. Small wonder, then, that most of the poorer population drank ale.

Bristol, especially in the poorer areas, was overcrowded and the population was rapidly increasing. In the year 1500, the City Kalandar Rolls estimated the number of people living in the city parishes to be around 4,900. The first attempted census of 1801 listed the population of roughly the same area as 40,000 and by 1831 the number of people living within the city of Bristol had soared to over 100,000.

The smell would have been dreadful, but worse, this was an ideal breeding ground for disease, in an era before the building of the great Victorian sewers which took everything underground and gave Bristol cleaner streets. In the 1820s, a conservative estimate put the annual amount of untreated sewage being discharged into the river Frome – open as it flowed across the centre of Bristol – at 20,000 tons. Many accounts of life at that time record visitors to the city not being able to cross the city centre without vomiting, so great was the stench.

Although people did not drink the river water, they used it for cleaning and other purposes, and rats and other vermin spread the bacteria from the river directly into the homes of the poorest and most vulnerable people who lived on the riverbanks and in the immediate vicinity of the rivers. Disease from the rivers and the overcrowded inner-city graveyards seeped insidiously into drinking water. Bristol, for centuries the second port of the land, now was reckoned to be the third unhealthiest place in which to live.

We know today that drinking water contaminated by sewage has always been one of the world's deadliest killers. In the Crimean War, more people were killed by disease than on the battlefield. In the immediate aftermath of the Boxing Day Tsunami in 2004 and indeed every subsequent natural world disaster, the highest priority was always to get clean drinking water to the survivors to try to prevent typhoid and dysentery. Even in England, clean drinking water was a vital rescue element in the 2007 floods. In the 1830s, there was no known link between contaminated drinking water supplies and disease, and in 1832 Bristol suffered its own disaster – cholera.

Asiatic cholera was not new. It had been endemic in India for centuries and indeed in one part of that country it had been worshipped as a goddess. However, the march of the British across India in the early part of the nineteenth century had brought with it new roads and railways, and areas which had remained largely undiscovered by the outside world, became accessible to the intrepid traveller, especially the pilgrims. And those in the cholera-affected areas were now able to travel much further afield too. Cholera also marched like the Empire but in the opposite direction. By 1830 it had reached Moscow and subsequently spread through Germany to England as it tracked the great trading and shipping routes.

Nothing prepared the English for the devastation of this most dreadful of diseases which could kill in a matter of hours. Although the more educated of the population had watched its progress towards them with horror, there was nothing to be done since no-one knew very much about it, much less how to fight it. Because it spread quickly through contaminated water supplies in the poorest areas of towns and cities, it provided indisputable proof to high-minded Victorian gentlefolk that those below them on the social scale were totally inferior.

Of course, most of the people who lived in the city also died in the city. Burial facilities consisted of the old mediaeval parish and churchyard burial grounds, a handful of noncon-formist cemeteries linked to chapels, and a few private plots near Broadweir. These filled up quickly, expanding the practice of removing their contents after an appropriate period of interment – usually to the charnel houses. This practice sat uneasily on the shoulders of the Christian church with its belief in the resurrection.

This system of disposal was severely tested in 1832. Before this date, although epidemics of disease were frequent, the introduction of vaccination against smallpox had at least relieved the situation. Then Asiatic cholera arrived.

Cholera first entered England through the northern ports which received boats returning from Asia, and for a while Bristol was safe. In 1832 the first case in Bristol was diagnosed at the old Stone Bridge, near Host Street on the north side of today's city centre (Host Street still exists), and the disease quickly spread around the slums where people lived in the most appalling, unsanitary and overcrowded conditions. Of the first 260 cholera victims, 168 were inmates of St Peter's Hospital workhouse. Burials quickly took place at St Philips and at Temple Church graveyards, where 31 victims were buried in one day. The only remedial treatment the citizens knew was to clean out the privies and lime-wash the inside walls of their houses. That apart, they crossed their fingers and put their trust in Divine Intervention.

Cholera is a complex disease affecting different people in different ways, although the basic symptoms are the same – high temperature and acute loss of body fluids resulting in dehydration, all accompanied by the severest stomach cramps. Sometimes the victim would become comatose and looked as if death had arrived, even when it had not. Occasionally victims recovered from this deathlike trance so it is not surprising, therefore, that people panicked. They were terrified. A rumour spread that paupers were being buried alive, and soon a crowd of angry and frightened people formed. In one episode they broke into a graveyard and exhumed the bodies to make sure everyone who had been buried was actually dead.

It became evident that the way to remedy the situation was to restrict burial in the city parish churchyards and other burial grounds and to find somewhere safer and cleaner for burial of the dead. To relieve this stress on the parochial graveyards, the Corporation purchased land near the cattle market adjacent to the river Avon. The high numbers of cholera victims being taken for burial continued to cause great concern in the city, and for this reason the dead were often brought to the cattle market burial ground by barge at night to avoid public notice. At least 584 people died in the epidemic – over a third of everyone who had been infected.

It was widely thought that cholera was airborne and that thousands of Bristol citizens were destined to die needlessly. But by the late 1830s, a link had been established between the unsanitary conditions in the area containing the old burial grounds and contamination of the wells providing the main water supply. This theory was later proved by John Snow in London and William Budd, an epidemiologist and the pioneer of public health improvements in Bristol. Budd was able to demonstrate that diseases such as cholera were spread by contaminated water supplies. His evidence was paramount in the enquiry which led to the Health in Towns Act although in terms of national acclaim Snow pipped him to the post by a few days because of a technical error in one of Budd's papers.

In 1836 the Bristol General Cemetery Company was formed and proceeded to set up The General Cemetery at Arnos Vale – near enough to the city to receive those who could afford the Victorian style of death, but far enough outside the city boundary to escape the wholesale closure of all burial grounds in 1854. All roads then led to Arnos Vale.

THE CREATION OF ARNOS VALE CEMETERY

AT THIS TIME, LARGE CEMETERIES WERE BEING ESTABLISHED IN MANY OF BRITAIN'S LARGER TOWNS and cities. In London, new cemeteries opened at Kensal Green (1831), West Norwood (1837) and Highgate (1839). This was in response to a social need and the arrival of cholera, but private cemeteries also presented a unique and safe opportunity for investors. After all, they reasoned, the only sure thing about life is death! Dividends could be as high as 8%. So let us not be too sentimental here: Arnos Vale, along with many of the other new cemeteries, was created by a private company for profit.

Private cemeteries were also becoming fashionable following the interest in them by John Claudius Loudon, a Scot, born in 1783. He was one of the first to recognise that cemeteries and churchyards provided a special historical record of life as well as death. When Kensal Green was set up in London, he proposed that several more cemeteries should be built at an equal distance from each other and from the centre of London, and he pressed for cemeteries to be laid out as botanical gardens and arboreta with heavy use of evergreens such as yew and cedar, but without flowers.

Loudon had been profoundly influenced by Père Lachaise in Paris. His major cemetery work, *On the Laying Out, Planting, and Managing of Cemeteries*, was published in 1843, written while he was in very poor health, and by that time he had become famous as a park and cemetery designer. He died that same year and was buried at Kensal Green. Loudon's radical suggestions for cemetery design and management were, in many ways, centuries ahead of his time. He moved for temporary cemeteries for burying the poor so that after they had filled up they could revert to farming land. He was an enthusiastic supporter of cremation, decades before it became an accepted practice, even suggesting that ashes could be buried under trees. This was, at the time, considered shocking and disrespectful and upset a great many people. However, there is no denying his influence on the great Victorian cemeteries, including Arnos Vale.

In 1837, an Act of Parliament enabled Bristol General Cemetery Company to set up The General Cemetery at Arnos Vale. The company had raised capital of £15,000 in £20 shares. Shares in Arnos Vale were promoted by the claim that the total burial area inside the city boundary was a mere 14 acres. The company bought 28 acres at Arnos Vale, built the Cemetery and opened it in 1839 at a cost of somewhere in the region of £16,000. The owners were astute businessmen who foresaw the day when the inner-city burial grounds would close.

Quite apart from the fact that the land at Arnos Vale was for sale at that time, there were several other reasons which influenced the choice of site for the new-style Cemetery. First was its topography, with the land curving gently around the shallow bowl of the hillside. The higher areas overlooked the city and would provide a spectacular and dramatic location for funerals. Second, its location – it was on a major road from Bristol to London, away from the centre of the city, but easily accessible for vehicles, particularly hearses. The Victorians were very impressed by all things classical, and here was an opportunity to create a truly beautiful and impressive garden cemetery in a wide-open space but with the hillside overlooking the city of Bristol.

The lower area of the Cemetery was set out as an Arcadian Garden which was visually very attractive and also represented a significant innovation in design. It is one of the best surviving examples in England and has Grade II status on the Register of Historic Parks and Gardens. It had a wide circular promenade named The Ceremonial Way, which survives today. This offered the novel concept that visitors might take a leisurely stroll around the area after visiting their family graves, a concept which is continued today in inviting visitors to Arnos Vale for tours and reasons other than simply dutiful visits to graves.

The Friends and the Trust frequently deal with correspondence from people who assume the spelling of the Cemetery's name should be Arno's Vale, not Arnos Vale. The area around the Cemetery was known as 'Arno's Vale' for many years before the Cemetery was created. A Peter Arno owned what seems to have been a gentleman's club there. Another explanation is that the whole district, which until the last century was very rural, was named after the river Arno which flows through the Italian city of Florence and the enchanting Tuscan landscape. The apostrophe in Arno's Vale was dropped by Ordnance Survey in the 1950s. All the signage in the city has also lost the apostrophe, and locals have long referred to the Cemetery as Arnos Vale.

Charles Underwood, one of the most respected architects of the time, headed the team which designed the four buildings. The two impressive matching entrance lodges, the Anglican Mortuary Chapel and the Non-Conformist Mortuary Chapel are all Grade II* listed and each demonstrates a different style of classical Greek architecture. They were built using the best materials and the services of the best master-craftsmen, which is why, despite decades of neglect and lack of maintenance, they remain standing – just!

The Cemetery was planted with trees noted in classical literature, including cypress, cedar, pine, yew, laurel, and rowan. In addition, the designers wisely kept the established oak and horse chestnut trees which were part of the original planting of the parkland estate and well pre-date the cemetery. The tall trees linking the areas behind the two chapels were planned as a theatre-like backdrop to the Arcadian Garden although their majestic effect has now been downgraded by the self-seeded ash and sycamore which fill every space and destroy the grassland. However, Nature also can be a gifted designer when left to her own resources, and the terraced slopes, originally landscaped in the style of an amphitheatre (for Arnos Vale was designed as a Greek necropolis) are now densely wooded and these woodlands provide an alternative backdrop: just as spectacular in a different way, particularly in the autumn.

There are very few images of how the Cemetery looked in those early days. Much of the landscape was grass, severely manicured along the pathways leading around the buildings, tombs and trees. It was elegant, calm and serene, and very open, giving a great sense of space. It provided a complete contrast to the overcrowded old graveyards in the city.

The Victorian attitude to death was very different to ours, and Arnos Vale offered a very fashionable place for burial. However, for many people there were problems. Its location, well away from the city centre, was a problem for many of the poorer classes, without their own transport. And, at the request of Dr James Henry Monk, Bishop of Bristol and Gloucester at the time, a clause had been written into the Act of Parliament reserving a fee of ten shillings for each burial in consecrated ground, payable to the Clergy of Bristol. This charge nearly doubled the cost of simple interment and put it out of the reach of ordinary folk. Thus, in the early years, business was very modest – no more than 25 burials in some years and the average for the first seven years is believed to have been fewer than 100. But everything changed when the inner city burial grounds and churchyards were closed, and Arnos Vale entered its golden era.

The Lodges, 1908

ARCHITECTURE

THE BUILDINGS

You are invited to turn off the busy A4 Bath Road, pass through the gates between the two Lodges at the main entrance to Arnos Vale, and enter an almost magical landscape.

The difference between outside – with the never-ending noise of traffic, buses and lorries thundering past, the car dealerships, supermarkets and fast-food outlets with their resulting litter, and the jumble of impoverished buildings – and inside, with its peace and greenery, is breathtaking. The visitor enters a different world – an oasis of green in a commercial, concrete desert.

The Cemetery is enclosed from the outside world by a substantial perimeter wall which clearly defines its boundary. The peace, tranquillity and serenity of Arnos Vale are enhanced by the buildings, carefully designed to complement the 'theatre' of the Cemetery gardens.

Originally these buildings set off to perfection the classical landscaping of the terraces and the Arcadian Garden. Majestic, without being over complicated or pretentious, the two lodges and the two mortuary chapels are buildings of immense importance, not only in Bristol but in the UK as a whole, since they represent a style of death and funerality which may never be experienced again. Of course, the original designers never intended the buildings to be set against a backdrop of wilderness, but they retain their elegance and beauty in this changed environment.

The four original buildings were designed in the Greek neo-classical style by a group of local architects led by Charles Underwood (1821–1868). It was a period of great British cemetery design, but even then Arnos Vale was regarded nationally as one of the most innovative and creative examples of its kind.

The architecture had to be right for a number of reasons. Firstly and most importantly, the buildings had to meet the requirements of a busy working cemetery in a major city. Secondly, they had to be in keeping with the overall design of the Cemetery, enhancing the environment for mourners and other visitors. Thirdly, if Arnos Vale was to win the kind of upper- and middle-class clientele the Bristol General Cemetery Company needed to maximise their profits, then the Cemetery, including the buildings, had to be fashionable. Although Arnos Vale was not designed by John Claudius Loudon, there is no denying that his influence was

A contemporary view of the Non-Conformist Mortuary Chapel

clearly in the minds of those who built the cemetery.

At the time of Arnos Vale's design, the most fashionable cemetery architects were drawing at least some of their inspiration from the Cimetière du Père Lachaise in Paris. It had opened in 1804, and was designed with an air of carefully planned, picturesque informality. At Arnos Vale, winding paths and carefully planted trees and shrubs fitted in with the aspirations of the English landscape designers of the era. There was also a nod in the direction of the traditional English rural churchyard – yew trees were not a random inclusion – with which the wealthier city folk would have been familiar.

Many cemeteries of the early nineteenth century have imposing entrances and most have one or two lodges at the entrance. Arnos Vale is no exception and its different architectural styles within the Greek neo-classical designs were used to denote the different levels of importance placed on each building. The East and West Lodges or gatehouses at the Bath Road entrance were built in the most basic style, the Doric order. They have very simple classical details, robust columns and uncluttered lines.

The lodges were designed to be the working buildings of the Cemetery and were home to the Cemetery Superintendent and his family. At one time it is believed that a member of the clergy was also resident. The lodges are linked by two tunnels (one inside and one outside) underneath the main drive-in area between them. One lodge also provided office accommodation where the business of the Cemetery was conducted. There was a Cemetery Registrar

An early view of the Anglican Mortuary Chapel

with an administrative office, and some basic facilities for other employees.

The two mortuary chapels were built to provide an appropriate architectural setting for Christian burial services. Two chapels were necessary – each of approximately the same size and quality of design but standing apart – in order to satisfy the requirements of both the Anglicans and the Non-Conformists or Dissenters as they were sometimes called. Separate provision was usually made in those days for non-protestant burials – Roman Catholics, for example. Adjacent to Arnos Vale is the Catholic Cemetery of Holy Souls. Most of the burials in Arnos Vale were protestant in the early days although there are some signs of other faiths in the non-consecrated sections, particularly in more modern times.

Interment in consecrated ground was not allowed without the rites of the Church of England, and all Non-Conformists steadfastly refused to bury their dead using any other service except that of their own persuasion. Thus Anglicans had their own chapel and were

The tomb of Raja Rammohun Roy: 'a conscientious and steadfast believer in the unity of the godhead, he consecrated his life with entire devotion to worship of the divine spirit alone, to great natural talents he united a thorough mastery of many languages and early distinguished himself as one of the greatest scholars of his day'

buried in the consecrated sections of the Cemetery, and the Non-Conformists, such as Methodists, Baptists and Congregationalists, had a separate chapel and the unconsecrated sections of the Cemetery for burial.

The great municipal cemeteries, which were set out after the legislation of the 1850s, often increased the number of chapels, with separate provision made for other faiths. Unlike Arnos Vale, these chapels were mostly accommodated in a single building, either sitting parallel to each other or housed in a T-shaped block.

The Non-Conformist Chapel at Arnos Vale was built in the sophisticated Ionic order of Greek architecture and was based on an earlier design of a Greek temple; more graceful and elegant than the lodges but still with sufficient moral simplicity to satisfy the austere beliefs of the Dissenters. Its columns have scroll-headed capitals and its elegant proportions are enhanced by its elevated position with an impressive flight of steps leading to its entrance doors. Other similar mortuary chapels of the day which survive show that the interior would have been graceful but simplistic, of lofty proportions and probably with fixed pews, and it was always described as being 'as cold as death' despite presumably having some basic heating. However in the late 1920s its interior was stripped out to be used as the new crematorium chapel and, sadly, there are no pictorial records to show what the interior looked like in its original condition.

Last, but most important to many of the Victorian benefactors, the Anglican Mortuary Chapel was built as the grandest of the four buildings. It is in a Roman Italianate style with shallow Corinthian columns and an arched and pedimented belfry stage. The capitals are beautifully carved with acanthus leaves and there is an imposing balustrade which encloses the

The General Cemetery at Arnos Vale

The beauty of a rare snowfall

The entrance to the first Garden of Rest with the Anglican Mortuary Chapel beyond

Peace and tranquillity in the early morning

These modern graves are of Bristol showmen

Looking west to the World War I memorial, with the 'Penny Memorial' in the foreground

The Anglican Mortuary Chapel half-hidden by unruly growth

The 1950s Crematorium Chapel with canopy and the Non-Conformist Chapel beyond

Springtime at Arnos Vale

Nature has her own way of dealing with neglect

A long-forgotten pathway comes to life with steps made by Friends' volunteers,
taking visitors from the lower level of the Cemetery to the grave of George Muller

Lady in waiting: the grave of Mary Carpenter awaits restoration

Living the high life in Arnos Vale Cemetery

The West Lodge following restoration in 2005

March 2006: Betty Utting (the wife of the last resident superintendent) cuts the
ribbon on the restored West Lodge where once she lived

7 August 2003: a day of celebration for the Friends as the care of the Cemetery is passed to the Trust

roof area on all sides. The chapel is set at the crest of two inclines enhancing its importance. In December 2004, the stunning cupola or bell tower had to be dismantled for safety reasons. The chapel interior, with its graceful curved windows, has marble wall plaques honouring the great and good of Bristol. It has fallen into sad decline but it will provide an excellent base for restoration, together with the replacement of the bell tower and bell. Visitors to the Cemetery can easily imagine a Victorian funeral procession following a horse-drawn hearse and carriages, with the bell tolling.

When laying out the burial grounds, the planners knew where the most desirable plots and grandest monuments were likely to be situated, and consequently they could plan ahead confidently knowing that those monuments would complement their landscape designs as time progressed.

THE MEMORIALS

Besides the four buildings, 25 burial monuments have been listed as being of historic and architectural importance at English Heritage's recommendation. Of these, the most significant, famous and definitely the grandest is the tomb or chattri of Raja Rammohun Roy, the celebrated Indian reformer and philosopher who died whilst on a brief visit to Bristol. In fact, so important architecturally is this monument that it has been given the coveted Grade II* listing, one of a select number of graves in the UK to be worthy of this status and one of only two in Arnos Vale.

The chattri is the focus of an annual pilgrimage on or about the anniversary of the Raja's death on 27 September 1833. Representatives of the Indian High Commission – often the High Commissioner himself – together with Indian and British visitors, meet at Arnos Vale to commemorate the life and work of the man who is widely known as the founder of modern India. The chattri is built of Bath stone on a plot which was bought by British businessmen William Carr and William Princep, both of whom had worked in Calcutta. Princep, an architect, designed the tomb. A further businessman, Dwarkanath Tagore, funded the building of the monument. The tomb was amongst the earliest in Arnos Vale and originally it stood alone in one of the unconsecrated sections of the Cemetery. The Raja's body rests in a brick grave beneath the chattri. Much is known about the life and work of Raja Rammohun Roy and this is, hopefully, a story for another day.

The design of the tomb is based on a traditional Bengali funeral monument, although the dedication plaque beneath the canopy was placed there later and, unfortunately, gives the wrong date for the Raja's birth. He was actually born in May 1772.

The second Grade II* listed memorial is that of Thomas Gadd Matthews, who was an importer of molasses and linseed oil but most significantly of materials used in the production of indigo dye. He was born in 1802 and he married Mary Leonard at Brislington Church on 26 August 1840. After their marriage they lived at Kensington Place, Brislington, which was the home of Mary's father, Robert Leonard. Brislington then was a much favoured residential area among the more wealthy citizens of Bristol, together with Clifton and Kingsdown. As Thomas's business prospered, he moved the family to other residences, and finally to Cosmo House at Portishead which later became the Bay View Hotel.

Mary's father, Robert Leonard, was in partnership with Thomas Gadd Matthews and both their names appear in the original Act of Parliament of 1837. They were also original share-holders of The Bristol General Cemetery Company. Her grandfather was John Hare who was a wealthy manufacturer of linoleum in the city and had endowed the building of Zion Church at Bedminster Bridge – another story, perhaps, for the future. The 'Church of the Vow' as it was also known, still stands but is now used as offices. Thus the marriage of Thomas and Mary brought together some powerful business names in Bristol, even though he was an Anglican and she was a Congregationalist.

In 1840, when the Cemetery was consecrated, the divide between the denominations extended into local politics, charities, business and burial. Burial law would not allow interment in consecrated ground without the rites of the Church of England, and all 'Dissenters' steadfastly refused to bury their dead using any other service except that of their own persuasion. In Arnos Vale the division was a visible one. Seven acres and a chapel were set aside for the use of all Non-Conformists or Dissenters, and the sections were originally separated by a sunken fence (so as not to spoil the view). Pathways between the two areas also marked the boundaries.

On his death, probably from a stroke, in 1860, Thomas was buried in the Matthews' new family plot in a quiet part of Arnos Vale. To overcome the divide caused by his and Mary's different religious persuasions, he had previously purchased what was to become one of the largest plots in the Cemetery and which lay across the edge of the consecrated Anglican section, and the edge of the adjoining non-consecrated section. Both areas were separated by a pathway which marked the boundary and which was then diverted around the edge of the plot. Thus he and Mary lie side by side, together in death as they were in life, but each in their preferred section of the Cemetery. Over his grave was erected the magnificent, ornate white marble memorial which he himself had commissioned before his death at a cost of over £1,000. It is his personal statement and, in the early days, it completely dominated that section of the Cemetery. A number of other members of the family are also buried beneath the memorial. The grave is guarded by a sentinel yew tree in each corner, a symbol of shelter to early Christians. The memorial's listing puts it on a par with the four cemetery buildings and the chattri of Raja Rammohun Roy.

Thomas Gadd Matthews' memorial crosses the religious divide

The visitor to Arnos Vale will immediately notice one of the features which sets it apart as a working cemetery from other more modern cemeteries: the diverse selection of monumental masonry.

Nineteenth-century memorials were influenced by famous furniture makers such as Chippendale, and, in addition, the closure of the inner-city burial grounds and the growth in the out-of-town new cemeteries with much more land gave a free reign to the monumental masons whose only display of their talent was actually on the graves of their clients. In Arnos Vale, a bit of 'one upmanship' is clearly evident, particularly in the forest of celtic crosses which sprang up all over the Arcadian Garden, many in rows and each cross getting larger as the row progressed.

The tallest celtic cross marks the grave of the Weston family and is located in approximately the middle of the original terraced area. Joseph Dodge Weston was born in Bristol in 1822 and became a successful industrialist, a City Councillor and four times Mayor of Bristol. In 1890 he became the Member of Parliament for Bristol East and it was no surprise, therefore,

The extraordinary Grade II memorial to Thomas Lucas

when he was awarded a knighthood for his services to the city. His illustrious career still touches the lives of citizens today, for he is credited with introducing the public library service to Bristol.

Given the dreadful state of dereliction which assailed Arnos Vale until 2003, it would be easy to suppose that a broken column had become a victim of neglect. However, this is not generally so, except of course where it is clear that the memorial has been vandalised, as the broken column symbolises a life cut short. The columns are usually in classical Greek architectural styles which correspond to the pillars on the Non-Conformist mortuary chapel and the gate lodges, that is, Ionic and Doric.

Many vandals have cast their shadows over Arnos Vale in many ways, and there is no more heartbreaking a sight than a plinth supporting a pair of tiny feet. This was a most appealing sculpture of a child angel which had stood for over 150 years guarding its grave and was broken off in an attempt, it is presumed, by unscrupulous dealers to steal it for resale to uncaring customers as a 'must-have' for their gardens with no thought as to its source.

Elsewhere the more traditional, simple cross, which was much less expensive and therefore more popular, adorns many a grave, including that of Mary Carpenter, one of Bristol's most significant social reformers. It is the ultimate Christian symbol, although many Dissenters felt it was too 'Catholic' and instead chose from the large range on offer at the time: for example, draped urns, lilies, weeping figs, broken columns and, of course, angels. In cemeteries and churchyards there are many lovely examples of angels, traditionally the Holy Messenger whose role is to intercede between God and humanity or to escort the departed to heaven. They symbolise spirituality and guard the dead and some carry flowers or even a child in their arms to represent the departed soul. The butterfly is also used to represent the departed soul winging its way to heaven.

THE GOLDEN YEARS

THE GOLDEN YEARS OF ARNOS VALE BEGAN IN THE MID-1850S WHEN THE HEALTH IN TOWNS ACT closed all the inner-city burial grounds and churchyards to decontaminate and protect the drinking water supplies. Burial plots were purchased 'in perpetuity' (forever) so the great Victorian families of Bristol assumed they were leaving behind a permanent monumental legacy which would remind future generations of their status and achievements in life. The cost of burial plots varied with the most desirable and expensive being those in the most accessible and visible locations – for example in the Arcadian Garden area or at the centre of the terraced hillside – so many of the grandest monuments can be found in the most obvious places. It is worth remembering that when Arnos Vale Cemetery was set out the site was already parkland, and the monuments now obscured by self-seeded trees would have stood proudly and prominently in the centre of the landscaped terraces.

The Victorian attitude to death was very different to modern times, and Arnos Vale offered a very fashionable place for burial. However, for many people there were problems. Its location, well away from the city centre, presented access difficulties for many without their own transport, and Bishop Monk's ten shilling levy did much to discourage ordinary folk from choosing Arnos Vale as the last resting place of their loved ones.

However, despite the expense and, for many, the inconvenience, of burials in Arnos Vale, the Cemetery began to fill up rather more quickly from 1847, when Bristol suffered a further cholera epidemic. A total of 778 cases were diagnosed, of which 444 were fatal.

During the 1850s, the public started to frown upon burial for profit and, in response, municipal authorities began to set up their own cemeteries. However, Bristol General Cemetery Company had enough political influence to prevent any major change in its status until the end of the century, not surprising, perhaps, considering how many mayors, lord mayors and other influential movers and shakers have their last resting place at Arnos Vale. During the period 1855–1890 the relationship between the Bristol Cemetery Company and the Corporation was 'interesting'. Although the City was empowered to levy a rate and establish its own cemeteries, it opted to make use of Arnos Vale instead.

Then, as now, the City was responsible for those of its citizens who died in poverty. Paupers from the workhouses, almshouses and the infirmary were buried in common, unmarked graves in the cemetery along with unchristened infants, bodies of those who had drowned in the waters around the city, and people who had committed suicide.

For some time Sir John Haberfield, who was one of the early Cemetery shareholders and six times a mayor of Bristol, was the Chairman of the Board of Guardians of the Poor and it was this Board which authorised the payment of burial fees by the City, to a company in which he held shares.

In 1855, the Health in Towns Act became law. This effectively closed all the old city churchyards and burial grounds and catapulted Arnos Vale into financial paradise when it became the principal place of burial for the people of Bristol. For nearly 50 years, Arnos Vale was to be a busy, hugely significant and extremely successful business. The passing of this legislation no doubt saved many thousands of lives throughout England, and its implementation was largely due to Dr William Budd, one of Arnos Vale's more important historical figures. In 1866, cholera broke out in Bristol again, but the massive public works programme which had been undertaken by then proved its worth, and only 29 victims died.

During these 'golden years', nearly all the most influential and important of Bristol's residents were at Arnos Vale. The monuments in the older parts of the Cemetery bear witness to the political and industrial importance of the city as Great Britain developed as a colonial power.

The number of people who lost their lives at sea is a testament to Bristol's importance as a port, and the number of social reformers show that many people wanted to narrow the divide between rich and poor, between men and women, and between the educated and uneducated.

The names of many prominent families appear on elaborate memorials. Members of the families of W D and H O Wills, who made their fortunes in tobacco, founded the University of Bristol, and employed thousands of people in their heyday, are buried in Arnos Vale. The Robinsons, another family of great industrialists in packaging, printing and paper-making, are also buried nearby. Among the 'ordinary' citizens resting there are survivors of the Charge of the Light Brigade and the Battles of Trafalgar and Waterloo, three Victoria Cross holders and a policeman murdered in the Old Market area of Bristol whilst intervening over the ill-treatment of a donkey.

In Victorian times, death wasn't the taboo subject it is today. Unsanitary conditions, lack of central heating, unrelenting childbirth, poor health and safety and, of course, terrible poverty, meant people often died young. Parents who didn't lose at least one child in infancy were the exception and young women regularly lost their lives in childbirth. Death was no stranger in the homes of the Victorians.

Of every 20 babies born, three would die before their first birthday and more before they were five. There are countless graves in Arnos Vale with monuments listing the names and ages of precious infants who died, one after the other. The rich may have been protected from the extreme hardships of poverty, and they may have had fine clothes and plenty to eat, but they certainly were not immune to infant deaths. As ever, things were worse for the poor for whom life expectancy was only about 40 years.

Many children's stories of the time reflect an almost obsessive preoccupation with death, but it's not depicted as a frightening or unexpected event. Of course, most people in Bristol at the time were Christians. They believed that, after death, they would be judged and, hopefully, go to Heaven.

A death in the family, although never completely unexpected, was inevitably a financial burden. As well as the substantial funeral costs, the middle and upper classes would be expected to provide a complete set of mourning clothes for those left behind, including the family servants. There would be a phase of deep mourning, with black being worn for weeks, months or even years. Queen Victoria, famously, never came out of deep mourning for her beloved consort Prince Albert and because of this, black became a fashionable colour. At the time of Albert's death, cemetery railings were painted black and many have remained so. At Arnos Vale there is evidence to suggest that beneath the black paint is the softer colour of green.

If a relative was more distant, or after a polite interval of time had passed, the relations of the deceased would go into a stage of 'half-mourning', wearing solemn colours such as dark purple or dark green trimmed with black.

When a person died, their body would be 'laid out', that is washed and dressed in their best clothes, by the undertaker and placed in an open coffin in the parlour or front room of the home. Curtains were drawn and clocks stopped. Mirrors were covered, and the body would be watched over at all times. Friends and neighbours would pay their last respects by visiting the deceased before the funeral and keeping their curtains drawn too. The lid would then be placed on the coffin and it would be taken to one of the chapels at Arnos Vale for the funeral service.

Less well-off people would have to carry the coffin themselves, or perhaps drag it through the streets on a wooden funeral cart.

It was a different story for the wealthy. A good funeral was not just a mark of respect to the deceased, but a way of showing off to the neighbours, much as a good wedding these days. Coffins were intricately carved and gilded. They were carried in an ornate, black funeral hearse pulled by horses adorned with black ostrich plumes and followed on foot by the procession of mourners. There were even professional mourners – known as 'mutes' – who would walk in the funeral procession looking melancholy and adding extra gravity to the situation. After the interment, lavish refreshments would be served. This was no mean feat given the potentially enormous number of mourners present.

The Cemetery Company charged for every little detail: nothing was inclusive. There was a fee of 1s 6d for tolling the bell of the Anglican Chapel and a further fee for a funeral held before 2.00 pm.

A postcard of the long funeral procession for George Muller, founder of Bristol's Muller Orphanage, shows hundreds of people, including the orphans, following the coffin through the city. The traffic is stopped and onlookers are going to extreme lengths to catch a glimpse of the procession – one man has even shinned up a lamp post. It looks as if the whole city turned out to watch the 80-carriage funeral of this much respected man.

If the funeral was for a child – sadly all too often – the mourners would wear white gloves instead of black ones. The horses would carry white ostrich plumes, and the child would be buried in a white coffin. Young mourners, especially girls and young maidens, would often wear white and the undertakers usually procured the services of a small boy (often from the local workhouse) dressed in black and complete with top hat, to walk before the hearse. Oliver Twist was not a figment of Dickens's imagination but an accurate portrayal of life at that time.

Those who could afford it would mark the grave with a stone or a monument, the grander the better. Some of the monuments at Arnos Vale are very impressive, made of the finest Italian marble or featuring exquisite sculptures.

Many of these sculptures are images which symbolised death. There is an amazing wealth of draped urns, scrolls, obelisks, crosses, broken columns, creeping ivy and grape vines, anchors, wreaths, lilies, passion flowers, clasped hands, doves, cherubs, angels pointing upwards and downwards and with trumpets, and weeping figs and willows.

There are a good many more unusual engravings and sculptures too. In the Arcadian Garden is a headstone with a carved pelican piercing its own body to feed its young on its own blood, illustrating that Joseph Williams gave his life as a doctor to save the cholera victims

The funeral procession for George Muller

whom he treated. Nearby there is a carving of a cat. A Baptist minister has his likeness carved on the end of his rather splendid table tomb, and a Sunday School Superintendent is depicted with a group of small children at his knee.

Around this time, the idea of cremation as an alternative to interment was being pioneered by Sir Henry Thompson (1820-1904) in the face of stiff opposition from the religious establishment which argued that burning bodies would prevent their eventual resurrection. Thompson was a surgeon at University College Hospital and a realist, and slowly more people came round to his way of thinking. The first cremation in England was carried out in 1885 by the Cremation Society at Woking.

In 1880 a further Act of Parliament incorporated more land into the upper terraces and the 1891 Act drew into the Arnos Vale Cemetery boundary an area which had previously been owned by the Maxse family and used as allotments and an orchard, and it became known locally as the 'top plateau'. This brought the total area of Arnos Vale to almost 45 acres – its present-day size. It is in this flat area to the south of the Cemetery that many working-class people are buried, particularly the railway workers and their families from Totterdown and Pylle Hill. One memorial to an engine driver carries a fine carving of his steam engine.

In 1897 the new Boundaries Act enabled the City Council to take over Greenbank and subsequently Avon View cemeteries and in 1900 pressure from some of the more affluent sections of the community, unhappy with the industrial expansion taking place around the Feeder Canal not so far from Arnos Vale, led to the City Council opening a further cemetery at Canford. The golden years of Arnos Vale were over.

THE TWENTIETH-CENTURY CEMETERY

ALTHOUGH OTHER CEMETERIES WERE NOW ESTABLISHED IN BRISTOL, ARNOS VALE REMAINED AN important part of life and death in the city for much of the twentieth century. When Queen Victoria died in 1901, after the longest reign in English history, the British Empire was at the height of its powers. The Empire had doubled in size during Victoria's reign and Bristol was still a very important port; but society was about to change very rapidly indeed.

In the first few years of the new century, the upper classes in particular continued to enjoy a life of pleasure and privilege. King Edward VII loved horse-racing and women. Indeed the Jersey Lily public house in Bristol's Whiteladies Road is named after one of his favourite mistresses, the actress Lily Langtry. However, by the time George V came to the throne after Edward's death in 1910, the storm clouds of war were already gathering on the horizon and, in times of war, public cemeteries acquire new significance and importance.

During World War I, thousands of young Bristolians left the city, never to return. Of those who did come back, many were seriously wounded. There were two designated military hospitals in Bristol, and the city was also home to the Gloucestershire Regiment.

The wounded were transferred from the front to hospital ships and then brought back to England. Many of those whose lives ended in Bristol hospitals had been transferred from the Mediterranean and landed at Avonmouth Docks. One of these military hospitals, the 2nd Southern in Bristol, had enough beds for 200 officers and 1,350 beds for other ranks. The Bristol County and City Asylum in Fishponds was converted into the Beaufort War Hospital, and many of Arnos Vale's World War I fatalities came from these two hospitals.

There are 356 World War I service burials at Arnos Vale. The Red Cross erected a magnificent Bath-stone memorial near the main entrance gates, on the site of the house built all those years ago by banker John Cave, to honour some of those who fell in World War I. It has four bronze plaques mounted in a cloistered walkway and in the triangular area of grass in front of the memorial are the mortal remains of many of those who are listed on the bronze plaques. There is a solitary marker stone to the memory of Sgt Henry Blanchard Wood VC MM, but at one time the whole of the area contained similar marker stones. These were removed for reasons unknown. Now, the whole area is beautifully kept by the Commonwealth War Graves Commission, who completed major refurbishment of the Grade II monument itself in 2006.

The World War I memorial with tablets as originally laid out

The memorial is known affectionately as 'Soldiers' Corner' and poppy wreaths are laid there for Remembrance Sunday.

World War I did not, after all, 'end all wars' and just over two decades later the city of Bristol was very much a part of World War II. There were a number of RAF stations and prisoner-of-war camps in the area, and as well as the military casualties of this war there was a high number of civilian deaths in Bristol.

Arnos Vale Cemetery is shown on a Luftwaffe target map dated 1940. The aircraft, flying from bases in France, followed the line of the Bristol Channel coast, turned eastward at the mouth of the river Avon and, it is believed, used the Cemetery as a sight mark for Temple Meads railway station and the Netham industrial sites.

A number of bombs were dropped in the adjacent districts of Knowle and Brislington and some actually landed in the Cemetery, missing the Non-Conformist Chapel by the narrowest of margins. Indeed, visitors admiring the graceful Ionic columns of the Chapel will notice the little square stone patches in them – repairs to the damage caused by shrapnel – and a closer

For valour. Henry Wood is one of three VCs buried here. He won his at St Python, France in October 1918 for leading an attack against enemy snipers. Daniel Burges won his in the Balkans in September 1918. His marble plaque was unveiled in 2006 and will be incorporated in a new memorial wall. The third VC is Gronow Davis

inspection of the memorials opposite the Chapel will reveal the chipped stonework. Local hearsay has it that the Cemetery was mistaken for a tented camp, but it is far more likely that damaged aircraft, or those with less resolute crews, released their bombs short of their target of Temple Meads railway station, a vital rail gateway to and from all parts of the country.

The bombs couldn't hurt the dead, but they decimated the living. The Luftwaffe was more interested in the works of the Bristol Aeroplane Company at Filton and the docks at Avonmouth than it was in the residential areas of the city, but nevertheless throughout 1940 a steady number of Bristol civilians were killed as a result of air raids.

As the year drew to a close, the German tactics changed. Recognising Bristol's importance as a city, the Luftwaffe was now charged with the job of eliminating Bristol as an important port supplying much of the Midlands and the south of England. On 24 November 1940, the Bristol Blitz started. On that single night 200 civilians died, nearly 700 were injured and communities throughout the city suffered terrible loss and destruction.

The graves of some of these, and others who died over the following months as a result of enemy action, can be found at Arnos Vale. Many are still remembered, and friends and relatives from all over the world recall the terrifying circumstances of their deaths.

On the military side, there are 149 burials from World War II at Arnos Vale. Some of these are gathered together in a small, sunny plot on the Top Plateau of the Cemetery, in an area set aside for the burial of sailors from the Naval Hospital at Barrow Gurney. Adjacent is a graceful Cross of Sacrifice – a symbol marking many World War II graves not only in the United Kingdom but all across Europe.

Right across the Cemetery can be seen individual war-grave markers on private graves. A choice was offered to the family of the dead to have the marker erected in a military cemetery or to have it erected on the family grave and many families took this second option. During the campaign to save the Cemetery from commercial development, these scattered war graves proved to be one of the strengths of Arnos Vale since the Commonwealth War Graves Commission rarely agree to their being moved. These grave markers are all in good condition in spite of the decades of neglect in the Cemetery, because they are cared for by the Commission, responsible for the graves of all the men and women who died in the service of their country in both World Wars. Many of the service men and women who so died are buried abroad in military cemeteries where they fell. Their names and the details of their lives and deaths are often listed on family headstones in Arnos Vale. This information is usually sufficient for family historians to locate their last resting place via the CWGC's database.

At least one of the World War II casualties buried in Arnos Vale died on active service in Bristol. Flying Officer Roy Rogers was training Flight Lieutenant Frederick Garvey in an Airspeed Oxford Mark I, based at RAF Lulsgate Bottom near Bristol – now the site of the international airport. As part of the training, the plane was required to take off and land at Whitchurch Aerodrome. Tragically, the twin engines cut out at low altitude resulting in the death of both trainer and pupil.

As the years rolled by in the 1900s, Arnos Vale Cemetery – ever popular with Bristol families as a last resting place for their loved ones – came close to filling up and as the land ran out so the income from burials dwindled. In 1928 the Bristol Crematorium was opened at Arnos Vale, using the crypt of the Non-Conformist Chapel to house the cremator and the chapel itself as the Crematorium Chapel. When it opened it was generally hailed as a state-of-the-art crematorium and initially local businessmen were invited to witness demonstrations of the cremator or furnace in action, usually by cremating a sheep. It was the very first crematorium in the West of England and, with its close proximity to Temple Meads Station, it received mortal remains from all over the West Country. So busy was it that a further chapel,

In front of the Cloisters stands the World War II Memorial for those who were cremated

waiting room with cloakroom, and an outside canopy, were added in the 1950s so that two services could take place simultaneously. Subsequently, two City Council crematoria were opened in Bristol and a private crematorium was also built in South Gloucestershire to the north-east of Bristol, resulting in over-capacity.

As society changed and adapted, and the lines between the social classes became less distinct, at least at the lower end of the scale, the memorials and graves at Arnos Vale reflected this change. The process of death became more democratic, but it also began to lose its status as an inevitable part of life. Death became an increasingly taboo subject – often mourners at a funeral were all male and certainly children were kept away. Memorials became much more modest in style and some graves were without headstones. Cemeteries began to lose their importance.

Of course people still came to Arnos Vale to be near their loved ones, to grieve, or just to reflect in the peace and tranquillity of the beautiful surroundings and views, but now in much smaller numbers. The process of change was well underway. The tradition of a loved one lying in an open coffin in the parlour was now less popular. As the century progressed, there were huge advances in health care and thankfully infant mortality decreased. The standard of living dramatically improved and people expected to live longer, so the living tended to distance themselves from the dead.

As ever, the graves and memorials of the twentieth century at Arnos Vale are reminders of the tragedies that befell Bristol and its citizens. They are a way of reminding us all of the air disasters, the great floods, the fires and the road accidents. But the graves can also remind us of the heroes and heroines, and the high points of life. One of Arnos Vale's most famous modern celebrities is footballer Billy 'Fatty' Wedlock, grandfather of the celebrated Fred ('The Oldest Swinger in Town') Wedlock, and one of Bristol City's most outstanding players ever, winning more England caps than any other player at that time. Centre-half Billy captained Bristol City in the club's only FA Cup Final – against Manchester United no less – and, after his death in 1965, few players came near to attaining his celebrity status or matching his achievements until the superstar players of the following century.

On the top plateau stands the memorial of the family of Trevor Stanford, better known to most people as the popular pianist, Russ Conway. His ashes were scattered at one of his favourite spots in Bristol, and his name is on the grave with those of his parents and brothers.

There are links with Arnos Vale right across the city. On the Cemetery terraces is the last resting place of James Hosken, the first captain of the ss *Great Britain*, Brunel's famous iron ship, now a firmly established and much admired Bristol landmark.

A large stone memorial tablet erected to the memory of Isaac Niblett can be seen in the foyer of Christ Church with St Ewen in the city. Niblett's name also appears in the 1837 Act of Parliament which set up the Cemetery and, as a prosperous man, he may have been an original shareholder. The tablet proclaims proudly that he is buried in Arnos Vale Cemetery and he does indeed have a rather splendid memorial on the lower terraces.

And no-one will forget having seen the majestic statue of Raja Rammohun Roy, which stands outside Central Library on land granted by Bristol Cathedral. The statue was given to Bristol by the people of India to celebrate 50 years of independence.

The closure of the crematorium in 1998 was the 'last nail in the coffin' of Bristol General Cemetery Company which then found itself with virtually no income, although it continued to bury in existing graves where space permitted and to receive ashes for scattering in the two Gardens of Rest from cremations now taking place in other crematoria. At the end of the twentieth century, the future for Arnos Vale looked very grim indeed.

A CEMETERY SAVED

By the mid-1980s, Arnos Vale, together with other Victorian cemeteries, had reached a critical situation. As they filled up, so the income from these privately-owned cemeteries diminished. Less money was available to pay staff, and new systems of rating reduced the revenue available for maintenance. Changes in social outlook had led to vandalism and indifference. The early Acts of Incorporation state that it is not the duty of the cemetery companies to care for individual graves and their memorials. There were fewer descendants left to care for graves, and in any case, sadly this became no longer a matter of any consequence to many. These cemeteries, including Arnos Vale, fell into a deplorable condition of neglect. Many of the once-splendid memorials were fallen and destroyed. Wind-born seeds of ash and sycamore grew into saplings, relentlessly invading grassed and burial areas, and bramble, bindweed and Japanese knotweed closed the paths once walked by visitors to their family graves.

In the later years of private ownership, maintenance of the burial grounds at Arnos Vale was mostly concentrated into a small 'presentation area' encircled by the once grand Ceremonial Way, although both Gardens of Rest continued to receive scattered cremated remains. The 'new' crematorium chapel built in the 1950s became a victim of fire (as did the little prefabricated chapel on the top plateau near the Cemetery Road gates) and funeral services at Arnos Vale reverted to the Non-Conformist Chapel.

Nine hundred years after William Rufus created the manor of Brisilton, and alarmed by a press report in 1987 that the private owners of Arnos Vale Cemetery had announced aspirations to clear away the graves and commercially develop a large section of the Cemetery, a group of concerned and caring local people came together to form The Association for the Preservation of Arnos Vale Cemetery – known as APAC. APAC became a member of the National Federation of Cemetery Friends and, encouraged by networking activities with groups at Highgate, Kensal Green, Nunhead, Abney Park, Beckett Street in Leeds, Sheffield and York, they campaigned steadfastly to secure a safe future for Arnos Vale and pressed the private owners to allow them to carry out voluntary remedial work to bring about some improvement. Not one of their many offers of help was ever accepted.

The reader here might be forgiven for thinking that there was little else to be done, other than to sit round a table and drink tea! However, that was not the case. The Committee met regularly and its members attended other meetings relevant to Arnos Vale and particularly City Council planning meetings, monitoring the threat of a planning application to commercially develop the Cemetery. The BBC made a film about the campaign and there were other parties to lobby and encourage to join the campaign; there were other Victorian cemeteries which had been at risk to visit and learn about. Other local groups generously offered display space at their own events. Many an afternoon was spent in Bristol libraries gathering information on the lives of those buried at Arnos Vale who had helped to make Bristol prosper. The local Member of Parliament was particularly supportive and helpful and even secured an Adjournment Debate. Saving Arnos Vale was news not only in the press and on television, but also in the House of Commons. No-one considered giving up, and doing nothing was never an option.

In March 1998 Arnos Vale Cemetery reached crisis point when, on the loss of their cremation licence, the private owners announced they were closing the Cemetery and locking the gates. In the event, bowing to public pressure, the office was closed, but the gates were left unlocked. It fell to the lot of a few dedicated volunteers to open and close the gates each day, a vital task with which they continue to be involved today since Arnos Vale is open every day of the year, even Christmas Day. In the same year, APAC changed its name to Friends of Arnos Vale Cemetery, a more succinct title which brought it into line with the other member groups of the National Federation of Cemetery Friends. However, the APAC logo, which was based on an embellishment on the grave of Dr Thomas Tovey Smart, has been retained on the Friends' stationery and memorabilia.

A group of volunteers stationed themselves at the Bath Road entrance to monitor any proceedings which might have threatened the safety of the Cemetery, and to be generally helpful to any visitors, following the closure of the office. A legal challenge mounted by the private owners' companies against the volunteers' vigil was dismissed in court. The campaign was strongly supported by the *Bristol Evening Post*, which reported continuously on the events organised by the Friends. A peaceful walk from the Cemetery to the Bristol City Council House was organised and impressively supported. In the best of traditions, Arnos Vale had once again stopped Bristol's traffic. The City Council announced that it would support the campaign, which then moved onto a different level.

And all the while the membership of the Friends grew and extended across the UK and then across the world with members in Australia, New Zealand, West Indies, USA, Canada and Europe. Regular newsletters produced by the Friends carried current news and details of ongoing work, not only to those who could also read about it in the press, but to those who had strong links with Arnos Vale but no longer lived locally.

In April 2001, convinced by the high and continuing level of public pressure, including a petition with over 20,000 signatures, the City Council decided to make a Compulsory Purchase Order, after the failure of negotiations with the private owners to buy the Cemetery. As expected, the owners lodged an objection, thereby necessitating a Public Inquiry, which took place in May 2002. Mid-way through the Inquiry the objections to the CPO were withdrawn, bringing the Inquiry to a sudden close. In October of the same year, the First Secretary of State finally confirmed the CPO. Incredibly, the owners still had a route of appeal by Judicial Review and right at the end of the year an application to the High Court for leave to challenge the confirmation of the CPO was applied for by the owners' companies. The hearing took place on 2 April 2003 at the Royal Courts of Justice in London and the challenge was dismissed. The Order was allowed to progress without further interruptions.

The legal processes of the CPO being subsequently completed, the ownership of the Cemetery land and structures passed into the hands of the Bristol City Council on 7 August 2003. Arnos Vale was out of private ownership for the first time in its existence – and saved!

In the meantime, the Arnos Vale Cemetery Trust had been set up as one of the recommendations of a Regeneration Study commissioned by the City Council. The Trust was awarded charitable status and on 7 August 2003, with the making of the CPO, the City Council exclusively licensed the Trust to manage the Cemetery on a day-to-day basis.

The Friends' volunteers were now free to work in the Cemetery, and have worked tirelessly and regularly the year round since that time, removing bramble and scrub, cutting grass and opening up pathways so that visitors can discover the treasures which have been hidden for so many years and family graves can be accessed and tended once again.

The previous private owners had also withheld the Books of Remembrance for the Arnos Vale Crematorium, and these had not been displayed since the closure of the Cemetery office in 1998, in spite of vigorous campaigning by the Friends and the Trust, supported by the City Council. Subsequently the previous owners sold these most sensitive of books to the *Bristol Evening Post*, which purchased them as part of its valued commitment to the community project to rescue and restore Arnos Vale Cemetery. For an interim period they were displayed in the foyer of the *Post*'s offices in Old Market Street in the city, and on completion of the restoration of the West Lodge they were given back to the Cemetery to be rightfully displayed as a lasting memorial to those who had been cremated at Arnos Vale.

The Books of Remembrance – there are five of them – are in a fragile condition, although they have been stabilised by Bristol City Council. They are not, however, in sufficiently good condition for new inscriptions to be added to them and the Trust has therefore purchased two new Books of Remembrance. Applications can now be made for inscriptions to be entered in them in memory of anyone who has a link with Arnos Vale Cemetery.

At the time of going to press the only matter to be resolved is ownership of the burial records. These most important of records, detailing all those who have been buried in the Cemetery, are currently the subject of negotiation between the previous cemetery owner and the City Council, since they apparently could not be included with the land and structures acquired by compulsory purchase. It is hoped that these negotiations can be successfully concluded in the near future, but in the meantime they are safely held in the City Archives and have been stabilised at the Council's expense to improve their fragile condition caused by unsuitable storage over many years. It is not currently possible for the Trust to conduct family history searches, but it is hoped that things will change on this front.

Arnos Vale once again welcomes visitors who wish to visit this oasis of quiet reflection and rest – a last point of contact, perhaps, to remember those no longer with us. Those parts of the Cemetery which have ceased to be tended regularly rapidly became a haven for wildlife. Particularly unsafe sections of the Cemetery have been fenced off. However, chestnut paling has been used to great visual effect and accompanied access is offered to those wishing to visit their family graves within the fenced areas.

Fundraising activities are organised regularly by the Friends throughout the year, with a vigorous participation in the Bristol Doors Open Day each September – part of the Heritage Open Days weekend organised nationwide by the Civic Trust. Heritage Tours of the Cemetery are organised and guided by the Friends. Details of all activities and events can be found on the website www.arnosvalefriends.org.uk

New Friends' members and volunteers are always welcome and membership application forms are available at the Cemetery or can be downloaded from the website. The Committee continues to meet regularly, organising newsletters (now mailed quarterly), fund raising events, tours and slide presentations. Friends' volunteers also staff the Visitor Reception Room at the West Lodge, welcoming visitors to the Cemetery, supplying information and advice, and caring for the Cremation Books of Remembrance.

OF THOSE WHO REST IN PEACE

WHEN THE HEALTH IN TOWNS ACT WAS PASSED IN THE MID-1850S, ARNOS VALE BECAME THE ONLY cemetery for Bristol and its surrounding area. It is not surprising, therefore, that it also became the last resting place for many of the city's great and good. It is not surprising either that, with well over 150,000 burials and approximately 120,000 cremations, this book could not hope to do justice to more than just a few. In fact, so many of Arnos Vale's residents have contributed to the City of Bristol that they could be the subjects of an entirely separate book, so perhaps a sequel may one day appear on the bookshelves.

Here is a brief mention of a few of those who sought to improve and develop the quality of life, not only for those who lived in Bristol, but for the population as a whole, even if some of them did not know it at the time.

WILLIAM BUDD MD (1811-1880)

There is no doubt that, of all the people whose life influenced the future of Bristol, William Budd ranks amongst the most important. He was one of the first to demonstrate the link between sanitary conditions, cholera and typhoid. His theories led to the preventative measures successfully used in the 1854 cholera outbreak, and his pioneering work was largely responsible for the successful passage of the Health in Towns Act itself. Unwittingly, he thereby promoted the shareholders and the Cemetery itself to a glimpse of financial paradise.

Budd was born in Devon and came from a family of doctors including five of his siblings. He studied medicine in Paris, Edinburgh and at the Middlesex Hospital, and he settled in Bristol in 1842, where he became a physician and lecturer. In 1847 he married Caroline Hilton and they had three sons and six daughters.

Budd's early intentions were to make the nervous system his life's work and he was always known as a very sensitive and caring man, but he was also attracted to chemical pathology, leading into the line of epidemic diseases, no doubt encouraged by suffering an attack of typhoid whilst studying in Paris. This, then, was the interest that led him into the wider field of sanitary reform. When he arrived in the city it was the third unhealthiest place to live in the whole country, but by the time of his death it had become one of the highest on the list of safe and desirable towns and cities in which to live. His evidence to the Royal Commission on

Health in Towns was to be his finest hour, having defined the difference between typhus and typhoid, and made the link between cholera, dysentery and contaminated water supplies. Undoubtedly, he would have found even more fame had not John Snow submitted his work on the same topic just a few days before Budd. The delay, caused by Budd's clerical error, cost him dearly but he was elected Fellow of the Royal Society in 1871.

William Budd's health declined in later life, possibly due to overwork and certainly to the stroke he suffered in 1873. He died at Clevedon, Somerset, on 9 January 1880 and five days later was laid to rest in the quiet terraced area of Arnos Vale Cemetery, where a modest headstone marks his grave.

William Budd

MARY AND JOHN BREILLAT

In the centre of the original area of Arnos Vale Cemetery, on the higher, terraced slopes, the visitor can find an impressive obelisk memorial built to the memory of Mary and John Breillat, both of whom have played a part in the history of Arnos Vale and of Bristol. When Mary died in 1839, the Cemetery was newly opened and hers was the very first burial – number 1 in the Burial Records. The grave is in a prestige position and, at the time of Mary's burial, there would have been sweeping views across the city to Purdown and the imposing Dower House on the Stoke Park Estate. In those days, plots in Arnos Vale were costed according to their size and position in the Cemetery, and this would have been an expensive spot.

John has a different claim to fame, as he brought the very first gas street lighting to Bristol. Having seen a demonstration of William Murdoch's gas apparatus in Birmingham, he was full of enthusiasm for gas lighting but could not get a sponsor, so in 1811 he mounted an exhibition of gas lighting at his own premises in Broadmead where he ran a print and dye works. At the same time, he placed gas lamps in the street outside, earning for himself the nickname of 'Brilliant Breillat'. Thus Bristol had some gas street lighting almost a whole year before the first gas lamps appeared in London.

Today, in the twenty-first century, it seems amazing that, in 1811, coal or town gas for heating was not even contemplated, and that citizens were so reluctant to abandon their smelly flickering tallow candles for such a superior light. Even Sir Humphry Davy, famous chemist and inventor of the miner's safety lamp, who began his illustrious career in Bristol, reflected the Victorian aristocracy's derision by sneeringly asking if the promoters were thinking of converting the dome of St Paul's Cathedral into a gasholder. John Breillat was undaunted, however, and rose to become chairman of his gas company. He died at his beloved gasworks in 1856, aged 81 years and was laid to rest with Mary at Arnos Vale. How fascinated he would have been, seventy years later, with the concept of a gas-fired crematorium at Arnos Vale.

MARY CARPENTER (1807-1877)

The poem of dedication on page 4 of this book came from the pen of Mary Carpenter, one of Bristol's greatest social reformers who was born over 200 years ago in April 1807. Mary's father, Lant (who drowned at sea in 1840) was the head of the Unitarian Church in Bristol at Lewins Mead. In those days, the Unitarians were not widely popular with the more conventional Christians because of their rejection of the Holy Trinity and the broadness of the movement. Charles Wesley, brother of the celebrated Methodist, John, and prolific hymn writer and preacher, expressed the distaste for Unitarianism in one of his hymns.

Mary was the eldest of six children and the family lived at No 2 (now No 3) Great George Street, just off the city centre. Dr Carpenter ran a very successful school, which attracted the sons of the rich and, unusually, Mary was a pupil alongside the boys. The benefit of Lant's excellent teaching techniques soon turned Mary into a teacher herself, and she worked with her father in his school, whilst also helping her mother run the household. 'I was early taught to be useful' was how she described her childhood and it was to stand her in very good stead for her later work of rescuing wayward children, particularly girls, for whom she passionately cared.

Whilst teaching at her father's school, Mary met the brilliant James Martineau and there is no doubt that she fell deeply in love with him. He had once been a pupil and, when Lant fell sick, Mrs Carpenter asked James to take over the running of the school. As a result of Mary's affections for him, her mother sent her away to be a governess on the Isle of Wight, presumably to introduce a little space between them. Later, Lant closed the boys' school and opened a school for young ladies where Mary did much of the teaching. The breadth of her education and teaching experience fitted her very well for her later work in India, where, amongst other duties, she trained teachers.

Mary was appalled by the plight of the poor and orphaned children around the notorious Lewins Mead and docks areas of Bristol, and was a frequent visitor to their homes. She founded a Domestic Mission in 1838, a free Ragged School at Lewins Mead in 1846 and the

Kingswood Industrial School in 1852. She published *Ragged Schools by A Worker* in 1849 and this took a hard look at juvenile offenders and 'the perishing and dangerous classes'. Her methods were often radical for the times, and she was strongly disapproving – and not afraid to say so – of prison sentences for children, especially girls. With funding from Lady Byron, Mary founded the Red Lodge (then called Red Lodge House) on Park Row as a girls' reformatory and lived next door in its smaller lodge as Superintendent. Her ragged school was, arguably, the first in the country but others swiftly followed her example.

In 1833, when Mary was just 26 years old, she met Raja Rammohun Roy during his ill-fated visit to Bristol. Mary had been extremely impressed with his work in India and later she would write *The Last Days in England of Raja Rammohun Roy* which she dedicated to 'Indians … who emancipating themselves from the thraldom of idolatry and superstition have devoted themselves to promote the elevation of their country'. Mary's concerns for the women of India stayed with her and in 1866, aged 59, she left for India on the first of four long visits, all undertaken in the last decade of her life. Her reform work for women and children became legendary and her name is still well remembered in India, where they came to call her 'Mother'. So well respected was she that Florence Nightingale invited her to visit, and she also took tea with Queen Victoria at Windsor.

Mary never married. Was her life too occupied and involved, or did her heart, once given, always remain with James Martineau who wrote the inscription on her plaque which was placed in the North Transept of Bristol Cathedral? Fittingly, this tribute to her is but a few yards away from the statue on College Green of Raja Rammohun Roy who so inspired her. However, Mary's real memorial lies in the changes and reforms she initiated in both England and India, and the concern and care she fostered in others to continue to educate girls, help prisoners, welcome students and work for a common humanity.

GEORGE MULLER (1805-1898)

George Muller lies in an Arnos Vale grave with an upright headstone detailing some of his work as the founder of the famous Ashley Down Orphanage. The simplicity of the memorial symbolises the simplicity of the man who worked tirelessly for over 60 years in Bristol, to provide a home and salvation to over 10,000 orphans. His obituary in the *Daily Telegraph* noted that he had 'robbed the cruel streets of thousands of victims'. He was a modest and God-loving man, but it was not always so.

Born in Prussia, George was a terrible rake in his young days. He was a highly educated undergraduate who swindled many people, including his own father, to finance his irresponsible lifestyle. It was only by the purest of chances that one night, with nothing better to do and having been in and out of prison for his misdemeanours, he went with a friend to a prayer meeting in a private house. He was profoundly affected and although his lifestyle did not change overnight, he gradually found the Christian way of life and prayer and came to England to train in missionary work. In October 1830 he married Mary Groves from Exeter and she was to provide the mainstay of his support for forty years. She had taken a chance on him, for she knew of his former life of dissipation, but together they made a strong team and loved each other deeply.

Mary and George moved to Bristol from Devon in 1832, together with their friend Henry Craik, and like Mary Carpenter they were deeply saddened by the plight of the hundreds of starving orphans living rough on the hard streets of the city, their numbers having been increased by a recent cholera epidemic. Within a few years, Mary had given birth to a daughter, Lydia, and then a son, Elijah. George and Henry worked jointly as pastors at Gideon and Bethesda Chapels.

Life was never easy for the Mullers, although their faith in God carried them through, and no more testing a time than in 1834 when Mary's father died in June and their beloved little son died four days later from pneumonia. Mary was devastated but George bore it stoically, not because he did not care but possibly because he could accept God's will more easily than Mary. She had no more babies, a surprising fact considering the average family at that time produced eight or ten children.

The orphans of Bristol were in George's mind constantly, and after the Poor Law Amendment Act in 1834 he determined to do something to save them from the workhouses where, if they survived at all, it was with no education and no skills to fit them for adult life, except perhaps those of the light-fingered variety. The feature of George Muller's achievements was that he never asked anyone directly for money, preferring to pray for what he needed. So he asked God for a house, cash and carers for the children and amazingly within a short time he had all three. The first orphanage was opened in Wilson Street, St Pauls, taking in 26 girl orphans aged seven years and upwards. Soon he had set up two further orphanages in the same street. Not surprisingly with 150 orphans living in three houses, there were bitter complaints about the noise, and still there were as many orphans on the waiting list as were housed by Muller so he wanted bigger and more suitable premises. He needed £10,000 and that was what he prayed for. After one month he received a gift of £1,000 from a single donor. Then, he received an offer to draw up the plans for a new orphanage at no cost. Incredibly things improved even more. He had found a suitable site at Ashley Down and the vendor suddenly offered to half the price if Muller wanted it for his orphanage. He paid £840 for it and by the end of 1846, his fund had received a further £9,000. In 1849 they all moved into their new 'stately home' which had 300 windows – one for each child. There were sufficient grounds for them all to play in, and they also worked in the garden growing produce to eat. Times had been hard in Wilson Street when often they were down to their last penny or loaf, and at Ashley Down it was sometimes much the same. But just as they thought they were at crisis point, someone would arrive with a gift of food or money and they would be able to continue. By 1870, four more orphan houses had been opened on the site, and a total of 2,000 children were living there. They were educated and well cared for, and provided the children abided by the rules, they had a good life. Even Charles Dickens paid a visit to convince himself that it was not a disguised workhouse and went on his way perfectly satisfied.

In 1870 George was beset with personal tragedy yet again when Mary, his wife of 40 years, died. Yet he still felt it God's will and in 1871 he married Susannah Sangar, whom he and Mary had known for many years. She proved a good partner for George in his subsequent lecture tours in Europe and North America. Earlier, George's daughter Lydia had married James Wright and together they had taken over the running of the orphanages, leaving George and Susannah free to travel.

Susannah died in 1894 and was buried with Mary at Arnos Vale, and four years later George joined them when he died at the age of 93. His funeral was probably the greatest ever witnessed in Bristol with orphans walking behind the hearse, followed by 80 carriages carrying an estimated 200 mourners. Thousands lined every part of the route and the traffic was stopped from the Centre to the Cemetery. It would have been memorable for the orphans, particularly as they had to walk back to Ashley Down from Arnos Vale after the interment. Over the years, ten thousand orphans found a home with George Muller and more than a million pounds had passed through his hands to care for them, all received through the power of Christian prayer.

WILDLIFE IN A CONSERVATION AREA

Arnos Vale Cemetery is a fragment of countryside in urban south Bristol, its plants and animals much appreciated by local people. Its ecological importance has long been recognised by Bristol City Council which has designated it a Site of Nature Conservation Interest. The Cemetery forms part of the Arnos Vale Conservation Area which contains no fewer than three cemeteries in close proximity, together with parkland and heritage buildings.

The woodland, scrub and grassland support over 300 different plants and trees – the paths are carpeted with primroses in spring and bluebells light up the shady woodland areas. Bird's foot trefoil, field scabious, ox-eye daisies, vetches, valerian and a host of others grow amongst the old tombstones in summer. There are some rare species too; for example, deadly nightshade, the nationally scarce ivy broomrape and white violets.

As well as fine mature native trees, several interesting and exotic trees and elegant shrubs survive from the original Victorian planting. Chestnut and oak have survived from the days before the Cemetery was set up when the site was part of a country estate and, of course, there is the dreaded Japanese knotweed, which has become the curse of many a Victorian cemetery in England and Wales. Holm oak (also known as holly oak because of its prickly leaves), Austrian pine, yew and araucaria araucana (a female monkey puzzle tree) survive from the early days of Cemetery landscaping. There are hornbeam, deodar and Chilean cedar too, which were introduced into Britain in the 1630s. Cedar frequently appears in classical legends and a preservative oil distilled from its wood was used in ancient Egypt for embalming.

Ivy should not be overlooked – it was the old symbol of everlasting life. It does not kill the trees on which it climbs, although it can smother a crown and its roots do compete with those of the tree for moisture in the ground beneath. Contrary to popular belief, however, it does not suck the goodness out of its host, using it only as a climbing support. It is one of the best of all bird-friendly plants, offering major benefits to them and wrens love it for its clouds of insects. Thrushes, house sparrows and dunnocks find security from predators in its secret depths. In autumn and in early spring, willow warblers and chiffchaffs feed amongst its dark green glossy leaves, and it is always a happy hunting ground for tits exploring the innumerable shady recesses for spiders, woodlice, earwigs and other delicious morsels, particularly in the difficult winter days. Its late berry season produces a winter crop when other store-cupboards are becoming bare. Its clusters of black fruit appear from January onwards and are great favourites of woodpigeons, mistle thrushes, blackbirds, song thrushes, redwings and overwintering blackcaps, not to mention flower arrangers!

Visitors to Arnos Vale Cemetery will catch frequent glimpses of holly bushes. Holly is a native of the British Isles and some of these may have been planted to enhance the landscape. However, holly is very much a symbol of Christmas and is extensively used in seasonal wreaths brought into the Cemetery in memory of loved ones at this special time. Ably assisted by the birds' recycling efforts, many of the bushes have been seeded from these floral tributes. We easily recognise the bright red berry, but how many of us know that it contains a single poisonous seed? Not good for us, therefore, but the birds' digestive systems cope very well, utilising the nutritious outer part of the berry, whilst discarding the seed complete with its own application of organic fertilizer. The berries last well into the coldest part of winter, a fact particularly appreciated by visiting fieldfares and redwings. However, the old adage that a good crop of holly berries forecasts a severe winter may be questionable, and is much more likely to be the result of a good summer past. A bonus is its provision of ideal nursery conditions for the caterpillars of the holly blue butterfly. Legend tells us that it is unlucky to cut down holly trees and they used to be associated with eternity and the power to ward off evil. No wonder holly goes hand-in-hand with ivy and its myths.

In early spring, bird song choruses are heard throughout the Cemetery, as at least 20 species get the breeding season underway. Summer visiting willow warblers, blackcaps, chiffchaffs and whitethroats mark out their territories alongside the resident woodpeckers, jays, thrushes, finches and tits. At least 60 species of birds have been seen at Arnos Vale over the last decade. As well as being an important breeding site, the Cemetery supports many unusual spring and autumn migrants as they stop off to rest and feed on their long journeys to northern breeding grounds or southern wintering areas. In fact, rare species of birds frequently select the Cemetery as their over-wintering refuge. And the visitor will scarce forget the early morning sight and deafening sound of a defending magpie and a grey squirrel having a set-to during the spring nesting period.

At least 25 different butterflies have been observed, their dancing colours lighting up the Cemetery from March to October. Pale yellow brimstones, small tortoiseshells, peacocks and commas appear first as they emerge from hibernation. Then come orange tips, laying their eggs on the delicate mauve flowers of lady's smock. Holly blues, meadow browns, gatekeepers, ringlets and marbled whites appear over the summer. Even the large orange and black silver-washed fritillary is seen most years. Soon the migrants arrive; red admirals and painted ladies, all the way from southern Europe and even north Africa. 2006 was reported to be a poor year for butterflies, but in the Cemetery they seemed to be in abundance. Arnos Vale supports good numbers of moths, dragonflies and molluscs too, and one important discovery is the rare cuckoo bee.

Animals are less obvious, but they are there; foxes, field voles, different kinds of bats, plus frogs and slow-worms. Visitors taking an evening tour may well be rewarded by the appearance of a fearless fox whose haughty expression clearly says 'Tonight this is my patch!' – a difficult act to follow for the hapless tour guide.

Arnos Vale is very much a living place for the natural world, supporting several rare and protected species as well as good numbers of more common ones. But everywhere, scrub, bramble, and coarse grass had taken over – a legacy from the past – leading to species-poor secondary woodland and a decline in the diversity of species.

Under an award from the Heritage Lottery Fund for the restoration and regeneration of Arnos Vale, a number of dead and diseased trees have been removed in 2007, together with many instrusive, self-seeded ash and sycamore trees, indiscriminately – and sometimes desperately – hacked down, and which have consequently grown into coppiced giants through a previous lack of skilled maintenance, wrecking beautiful monuments and desecrating graves and tombs. This removal work has been carried out by professional tree management contractors, supported by the ongoing work of the volunteers of the Friends of Arnos Vale Cemetery who, together with other volunteer groups, have brought about such a visual difference in all parts of the Cemetery.

With careful management, sensitive to the needs of visitors to the graves of loved ones, much of the grasslands can be restored, allowing some scrub and woodland to remain. After initial tree removal, carpets of primroses magically appeared, cascading down the once darkened slopes that line the main carriageway linking the Bath Road and Cemetery Road entrances. Already Arnos Vale promises to take its place in Bristol as a beautiful cemetery: a calm, peaceful and harmonious refuge for both people and wildlife.

FACING THE FUTURE

Twenty years before this book was written, the future for Arnos Vale looked perilous and hopeless, and to many it seemed horrific, but over two decades the campaign to save and restore the Cemetery has reached a height never envisaged by any of the early campaigners. When APAC was founded, its aims included keeping the gates open and protecting the graves and headstones. A bonus would have been permission to carry out work to improve the pathways and stop some of the dereliction. Thanks to 'people power' and a tenacity which probably has not been experienced in Bristol since the end of the World War II, the Friends of Arnos Vale Cemetery sowed the seeds of a safe future for the Cemetery which have been nurtured and cultivated by the increasing involvement of other organisations. The Arnos Vale Cemetery Trust was set up in 2001, and the founder Trustees helped to shape the regeneration plans with the City Council, culminating in a Compulsory Purchase Order in 2003.

When the City Council licensed the Trust to take over the day-to-day management of the Cemetery following the CPO, the Trust assumed responsibility for the more regular activities of a cemetery, i.e. burial of mortal and cremated remains and the scattering of cremated remains in the two Gardens of Rest, since Arnos Vale continues to be a working cemetery. Gradually expanding from a point where a few people did everything on a voluntary basis, the Trust now has two full-time employees with plans for more in the future.

In December 2005 the Trust, in partnership with Bristol City Council, received an award of £4.82 million from the Heritage Lottery Fund. This was conditional on a further sum of over £600,000 being raised as match funding – a huge task in days when there are so many worthy causes all having to ask the public at large for funding because there is insufficient, it seems, from governmental coffers. Using a professional fundraiser appointed by the Trust, good progress has been made in reaching this target, although there is still a way to go yet. Match funding can also consist of volunteer hours – time worked by volunteers in the Cemetery on a variety of tasks to help its improvement.

Work is now well underway to preserve and restore Arnos Vale and the plans for the future are ambitious and exciting. The work includes complete restoration of all four Grade II* buildings – no mean feat in itself – together with improvement to the burial grounds to turn the decades of neglect into a 'managed wilderness' where visitors can stroll in safety and appreciate the peace, the birdsong and flora, and all just a stone's throw from a twenty-first-century concrete city centre.

Arnos Vale will become Bristol's Social History Landmark – for the people. Some of the Victorian landscape will be revealed but there are no plans to 'manicure' this important wildlife site out of existence for, after all, the importance of this green urban area helped to save Arnos Vale from development.

Restoration of the West Lodge, at the Bath Road gates, was completed in 2006, thanks to the support of English Heritage and including a donation of £10,000 raised by the Friends. For years it stood crumbling, derelict and sad, shrouded in protective scaffolding and plastic sheeting and suffering serious deterioration, with collapsed upper floors and a roof which must have been held together only with spiders' webs. It now includes a busy Visitor Centre, and currently houses the Crematorium Books of Remembrance. It is staffed by Friends' volunteers during the times when it is open to the public.

Its twin, the East Lodge, on the opposite side of the entrance gates has also suffered serious damage due to neglect, even though scaffolding and plastic sheeting have been employed in an effort to try to slow down the deterioration. Future plans for this building include a basement area where the Friends' volunteers can meet, store tools, eat their packed lunches and enjoy a well-earned cup of tea on the days when they are working in the Cemetery. The entrance (middle) floor may provide accommodation for family history researching, and upstairs the three offices, previously converted from bedrooms, will be refurbished for some of the employees of the Trust.

The Anglican Mortuary Chapel has also suffered deterioration, but the bell tower, dismantled for reasons of safety in 2004, will be restored and replaced, together with its original bell. The chapel will provide a facility to hold funeral services even though cremation or burial may take place at another location. As all the buildings have to earn their keep once they have been restored, it is also planned to offer the chapel as a venue for exhibitions, musical recitals and other appropriate activities.

The Non-Conformist Chapel will become an education centre and the hub of Arnos Vale's future activities, with the appointment in due course of an education officer. Courses will be run in conjunction with schools for young students to learn about the heritage of the City of Bristol and the unique wildlife haven which Arnos Vale has become. Adult students will also be catered for, with courses and lectures to suit demand. There will be wheelchair access to this building, enabling all to use it in spite of the steep approach steps, and there will be public toilets too.

A glass entrance lobby will be added to the west side of the Chapel where visitors may enjoy a coffee or tea and sit awhile there or, when weather permits, out on the terrace which will extend over the roof of the ex-crematorium which was located underground – a great improvement. This new addition will be discreetly screened by the large yew tree which grows alongside the chapel steps.

The small crematorium chapel, its adjacent waiting room and the useful but rather ugly canopy in front, built mainly in the 1950s, will be demolished. In their place it is planned to build a Remembrance Wall, which will display memorial plaques. Just around the corner, the Cloisters and World War II memorial will be retained and refurbished. There are no plans to alter the two Gardens of Rest where cremated remains have been scattered for eight decades.

Some work on the burial grounds has already taken place, with dead or diseased trees removed, together with many of those self-seeded ash and sycamore, which cause so much damage to graves and masonry. Careful pruning of the original trees and those which pre-date the Cemetery will, it is hoped, prolong their life. As the areas have been opened up, so the dark patches of moss and scrub have given way to young grass and wild flowers such as primroses, all set free in the sunlight and playing their part in the restoration of Arnos Vale. There will be further improvement work to the pathways and particularly the main carriageway through the Cemetery which links the Bath Road gates to those at Cemetery Road. Temporary pothole filling has taken place over the last few years, but the huge craters, which made the road so hazardous to both pedestrians and vehicles alike, will be a thing of the past.

There will be some major upheaval during the restoration work, but the Trust will take every measure it can to protect existing masonry and keep pathways open whilst they are being improved.

The Friends of Arnos Vale Cemetery are now preparing to enter their third decade, knowing that projects which could only be dreamt about in the past will become reality in two or three years. Events and fundraising will continue in order to expand on the regeneration programme funded by the HLF. Projects such as an improvement to the grave of Mary Carpenter, which is not listed and will not be eligible for lottery funds, are already in hand and the opening up of more pathways will reveal further treasures for visitors taking the ever popular wildlife and heritage tours.

In October 1840, *Felix Farley's Bristol Journal*, reporting on the Consecration of Arnos Vale Cemetery by Bishop James Henry Monk, recorded:

> The beauty of the morning attracted a large concourse of spectators including our resident fashionables. We think we may in all safety predict, when all arrangements are completed, the grounds planted, the various tombs and memorials erected, that few if any cemeteries in the kingdom will surpass the Cemetery at Arnos Vale.

Arnos Vale Cemetery now has a secure future, which means that already some of the early aims of the Friends have been achieved. Working together with the Trust and the Bristol City Council, the Friends are confident that with the help of those who care, Arnos Vale will once again achieve the respect, dignity and prestige which attended its inception.